PASSIONATE BELIEVING

By the same author:
The Unseen Face of Islam

Passionate Believing

BILL MUSK

MONARCH PUBLICATIONS
Tunbridge Wells

ISBN 1 85424 172 9

Unless otherwise indicated, biblical quotations are from the
New International Version © 1973, 1978, 1984 by the
International Bible Society.

All Qur'ânic references are taken from
A. Yusuf Ali *The Glorious Qur'an*
American Trust Publications 1977.

Production and Printing in England for
MONARCH PUBLICATIONS
Owl Lodge, Langton Road, Speldhurst, Kent TN3 0NP
by Nuprint Ltd, Harpenden, Herts AL5 4SE.

ACKNOWLEDGEMENTS

I am grateful for the stimulating suggestions of Kenneth Cragg and Charl le Roux in my initial investigation of 'Islamic fundamentalism'.

My thanks are due to several people for their expert reflection on various parts of the developing text: Nabeel Jabbour, Arthur Jones, Philip Lewis, Malcolm Steer and Sam Yeghnazar. I am indebted to Colin Chapman and Vivienne Stacey for their review of the whole manuscript and their suggestions as to how it might be improved. The mature text is hopefully accurate in detail and reasonable in reflection. Any errors of fact or judgement are, however, mine alone.

My wife Hilary has also reviewed the whole manuscript. With her encouragement I have decided to let the text flow in English with technical Arabic terms relegated to parentheses, or at the very least properly explained. I am sure that the book 'reads' much better as a result and I am thankful for her support and enthusiasm for this project!

Sheila Stenson, librarian at Maghull Library, helped facilitate my research, procuring all kinds of books for me, and for her assistance I am grateful.

The members of St Peter's, Maghull, have been very gracious in allowing me space to pursue this area of interest while I have been their vicar! To them go my love and thanks.

I have appreciated the encouragement of Tony Collins and Lizzie Gibson of Monarch Publications in urging me to write on this delicate and relevant subject.

CONTENTS

LIST OF FIGURES

PREFACE

'Passion and prejudice govern the world,
only under the name of reason.'

John Wesley

Do you remember those television clips from the funeral of
Ayatollah Khomeini? Millions, literally, of Iranians crowded
their capital city to glimpse and, if possible, touch the corpse
of their beloved Leader. Only a helicopter prevented the
body from being ripped to pieces. The mass hysteria was a
little different from the solemn atmosphere at the state
funeral of Sir Winston Churchill!

If you were an Iranian you might recall television clips
from the days of the so-called 'hostage crisis'. Night after
night, fresh revelations were published implicating American embassy officials in the maintenance of the oppressive
regime of the hated Shah. What had a distant superpower
been doing, promoting so strongly the degradation of a
Middle Eastern state? The students had every right to take
over the embassy and its wicked occupants! Long live the
Islamic revolution!

Passion is highly visible in declarations about 'Islamic
fundamentalism'. 'Supporters' and 'opponents' feel very
strongly about the subject. Less visible and more subtly
present is prejudice. The contentions and counter-conten-
tions are prejudged from particular standpoints, both for and
against. All contenders, of course, feel that they are being
perfectly reasonable!

The aim of this book is to delve into those various passions and prejudices and discover their foundations. What,
exactly, is 'Islamic fundamentalism'? Who are the
'fundamentalists'? In what contexts have these radical move-

ments for change occurred? Why is 'Islamic fundamentalism' in such high profile and such widespread manifestation today?

The uncovering of basic 'Islamic fundamentalist' themes produces a few shocks for the Western researcher. We soon discover that Westerners cannot remain simply observers of a phenomenon belonging to strangers, those peculiar Muslims. The truth emerges that Westerners and Western culture have actually helped inflame and energise 'Islamic fundamentalism'. The exposition of major facets of the 'Islamic fundamentalist' outlook on life leads intriguingly to a questioning of our own outlook on life. If questions of the goose are fair enough, so are questions of the gander!

Reasonably informed and excited minds need to come to the bar of Scripture. What light do Old and New Testament throw on the perennial issue of how to evaluate human cultures? Are there some guidelines given by God that apply to all human societies in all ages? Where, by contrast, does the divine Creator exult in a kaleidoscope of cultural variety? Does 'Western culture' approximate more to a biblical ideal than that envisaged by 'Islamic fundamentalism'? Perhaps we all need to acknowledge certain built-in passions!

'Passion' can have good connotations as well as bad. Behind the rhetoric lie commitments made by human beings, commitments for which some are quite willing to die. Britain had her 'finest hour' in a struggle against a Führer and a Reich which she perceived as evil. The motivation of many Muslims today, though quickly dismissed by the Western media as 'militant fundamentalism', may not be far different, at least in their own eyes. We must probe gently into others' lives.

The material presented in this book falls into three major sections. First, the subject of 'Islamic fundamentalism' is introduced and explained. The aim in such explanation is to help us grasp, from the Muslim's perspective, how life should ideally be organised. We need to note that a variety of 'insider' terms, including 'reformist Muslim', 'resurgent Muslim' and 'Islamist', refer to the same kind of person: the person we, from outside, have grown accustomed to labelling 'Islamic fundamentalist'. From the inside, that person considers himself to be a Muslim who longs to live in a God-ordered society, subject to Islamic law. The chief proponents or ideologists of such a way of looking at life are termed 'visionaries'.

The second section of the book presents significant historical and contemporary models of 'Islamic fundamentalism'. The biographies and country studies in this section illuminate the force of the reformist manifesto. Individuals, regimes and nations have been transformed as a result of its appeal. The case histories of Pakistan, Egypt and Iran are deliberately chosen for several reasons. They include the major ideologists of this century's expressions of 'Islamic fundamentalism'. They portray the early development of such 'fundamentalist' thinking in the subcontinent of India. They illustrate the difference of approach between Sunnî and Shî'a sects to resurgence. They proffer contrasting stories of the development of Islamism, highlighting a variety of models of 'fundamentalism'. Those models differ as a result of the particular contexts in which they developed.

The third part of the book offers evaluation and reflection. What is the nature of 'authority' in Islam? How can movements for reform be permitted or accommodated or even endorsed? How do non-'fundamentalist' Muslims view the Islamists? Indeed, what possibilities are there for reformist Muslims to find a niche which they would accept in any society other than the 'government of God' espoused by themselves? What hope is there in a secularised country like Great Britain for easy accommodation of resurgent Islam? What possibility of national harmony is there in a complex country like Iran, now firmly established around reformist principles?

What does our look at 'Islamic fundamentalism' expose concerning a 'fundamentalist' attitude hidden deep in our own Christian sub-cultures? Can the Bible help us find our way in this most sensitive of areas?

Throughout the book are interspersed brief encounters with 'Islamic fundamentalists': girls in prison, guerillas on a highway, a preacher on a bus, a boy in a hearse. These imaginary pieces are built on observation and primary sources. Hopefully they take us beyond theory to the convictions and life-goals of real people.

Appendices are added which offer an explanation of Arabic transliteration, an introductory bibliography, a glossary of terms used and some explanatory notes.

Missing from the text is a studied suggestion as to how Islamists may most appropriately be reached for Christ. It seems to me that Western Christians have first got to come to terms with the real, complex issues lying behind 'Islamic fundamentalism'. With a few notable exceptions, effective witnessing to Islamists remains a future dream.

My prayer is that this book will assist Western Christians in understanding how 'Islamic fundamentalism' makes sense to many modern Muslims. If we can patiently sift others' passion and prejudice, we may come to a better comprehension of their point of view. Such comprehension may lead to a deeper empathy with the people concerned. Listening as we read may also throw some light onto our own blinkered perspectives. Perhaps we shall be provoked to repent of some of our ethnic, confessional or personal prides and prejudices.

Most of all, I pray that the Holy Spirit might encourage us through these pages to trust him more fundamentally. He alone can accurately judge the motives of human hearts: Western, secularist or 'Islamic fundamentalist'. He is the one like the wind, blowing where he will: in post-Revolution Iran, northern Nigeria or pluralist Britain. He supremely can replace a spirit of fear with love that remains serene in the midst of hostility. His greatest tale is one of incarnation, of the wheat falling into the ground to die on others' behalf. With his help, Christ's mind can become ours as we get to know the 'Islamic fundamentalist', our fellow human being. From a secure servanthood might arise creative ways of sharing the heart of the gospel with people for whom that heart is a missing and much-needed centre.

Bill A. Musk

PART 1

CHAPTER ONE

I'M SORRY, I'LL READ THAT AGAIN!

Tasty Jesus!

FOR MANY MONTHS OF HER INFANT LIFE our third daughter Sarah thought that Jesus was edible; what's more, he tasted good!

We were living in Egypt where, every January, Coptic Orthodox Christians celebrate Epiphany as a special festival.[1] Part of the merrymaking consists of making, or buying readymade, a cake delicately constructed from fondant icing. The cake depicts a crib scene with the infant Jesus being visited by shepherds from the hills around Bethlehem and wise men from the East. Jesus is, of course, made out of icing.

In January 1985, Sarah had reached that stage where she was grasping new words and ideas daily. It was Epiphany time and an Egyptian friend had bought for us an Epiphany cake, including, of course, a fondant 'Jesus'. Now it just so happened that during the Christmas of that winter our little girl had learned the carol 'Away in a manger'. The first verse was fixed firmly in her head. It includes the statement: 'The little Lord Jesus lay down his sweet head.' Everything fell into place: Jesus the ultimate gob-stopper!

The information appreciated audibly—the carol—and

17

the stimulation received visually and via the tastebuds—the cake—combined to confirm in our daughter a specific way of looking at the concept 'Jesus'. In a simple way Sarah was doing what we all do all of the time. She was looking out on the world (in her case the 'Jesus' world) from her own limited stock of assumptions and concepts of reality.

Looking out

How do we look out upon the world? What do we 'see'? Do we all 'see' the same? Figure 1 illustrates the point of such questions in a simple way. Glance quickly at the drawing. What did you see? A vase? Look again. Two faces looking at each other? You could have seen either, for both are deliberately there.

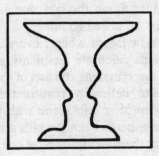

Figure 1
What do you see?

The same external stimulus can be looked at in different ways. People studying the same outline of ink on white paper could formulate very different conclusions as to what is represented there. Both would be correct in their descriptions of what they 'see'.

Most of us 'see' and enjoy colour. Colours are a wonderful gift in the world of light in which we are immersed. However, colours are not permitted to remain neutral, simply decorative. They are coded and put to use to convey unspoken commands, warnings or other messages.

We who are British by birth and residence are taught, for example, the important significance of red (danger) and green (all clear). It wasn't until my family came to live in Merseyside that we learned the true connotation of red versus blue. Everything here seems to be conditioned by that colour comparison. As editor of our parish magazine I quickly learned that if one month's cover is blue (the colour of Everton football club) then the following month's cover must be red (the colour of Liverpool football club).

In the Muslim world of the Middle East one soon discovers that green and gold are special, almost 'holy' colours. In Afghanistan, don't paint something yellow if you want it to appear attractive! Yellow, in that cultural context, carries a different connotation. By contrast, for North Americans, the colour yellow evokes the sentiment 'please come safely back'. The song 'Tie a yellow ribbon round the old oak tree' is a culturally-agreed symbol for affirming that the homeland is waiting, remembering, praying.

Looking out is done through eyes that have been taught to wear the appropriate culture's spectacles.

Looking in

Perception of meaning in colour, then, is strongly conditioned by our cultural background. Getting the point of jokes is even more dependent upon our cultural heritage. Humour revolves around the unsaid or the implied in a recounted situation. The listener has to be able to imagine the complete context in order to laugh at the peculiar situation being portrayed. Jokes are shorthand comments on the behaviour of people in a commonly understood milieu.

My wife and I never did catch on to Lebanese humour— was this because of the Lebanese/French connection we ask ourselves? Egyptian humour, however, seemed much more our cup of tea; especially the 'Saʿîdî' jokes. We loved those.

As soon as you leave Cairo travelling southwards, you are in Saʿîdî territory. You are in the realm of the traditional Egyptian, the peasant farmer, the southerner, the country bumpkin:

> There were three Egyptians convicted of a terrible crime and condemned to death. One Egyptian came from Cairo, one from Alexandria and the third from the Saʿîd. On the day of their execution they were each given the choice of death by hanging, death by firing squad or death by guillotine. The Cairene was asked first and he chose the guillotine. As the blade descended towards his neck it suddenly stopped: it was an obvious act of God and the man was allowed to go free! The Alexandrian was asked next and he also chose the guillotine. As the blade descended towards his neck it again suddenly stopped: another act of God and the Alexandrian walked free! The executioners then asked the Saʿîdî which method he would like to choose. 'I'll take the firing squad,' he exclaimed, 'that thing doesn't work properly.'

Maybe the joke is familiar but with substitutes for the Cairene, Alexandrian and Saʿîdî? It plays upon a majority's stereotyping of a certain subgroup of people within a particular nation. You have to know the characteristics of that people, or be able to relate them to a similar perspective within your own background, in order to 'get' the joke.

Humour has to do with what is implicit in our outlook upon the world. Most good comedians within a specific people group are adept at pointing out the absurdities in the attitudes or customs of that group by the process of exaggeration.

Comedians ask, for example, 'Aren't we British just a little bit over-the-top with our stiff-upper-lip-in-the-face-of-all-adversity?' 'Isn't our concern for pets sometimes rather out of proportion considering our inability to relate healthily

to our own human family members?' 'Isn't it a little absurd
for the Englishman overseas to expect the rest of the world
to understand and use his language? And if there is any hint
of non-understanding is it really appropriate simply to shout
the Queen's English more loudly?'

We all laugh, knowing that the joke is on us—on our
culturally learned way of looking at life. Yes, perhaps we are
a little ridiculous sometimes!

Kneeling or standing?

All human beings have basic biological, psychological, socio-
cultural and spiritual needs. We all need food to survive. We
all look for some kind of meaning in life. We all operate with
language as a major means of communication. We all (from
a biblical perspective) have some kind of innate leaning
towards concepts of supracultural beings, the traces of the
image of God in us.

How such basic needs are expressed and how they are
satisfied varies infinitely from culture to culture, even from
family to family or individual to individual. In each of the
areas of basic human need, however, there are considerable
degrees of consensus according to whether one is Westerner
or Middle Easterner, British or Arab, Anglican or
Orthodox.

Westerners, for example, exist in a secular society; Middle
Easterners live in a religious world. British people prefer to
live in nuclear family units; Arabs tend to live in extended
family relationships. Anglicans kneel, sit and stand politely
for worship; Orthodox come and go during their church
services, standing throughout.

We tend to learn to look at life in the same kind of way
that our parents looked at it. From the moment we are born
we are subject to an all-encompassing but unannounced
programme of cultural conditioning. This is what you wear.

That is how you sit. This is what you eat to stay healthy. That is what you say to show you are polite.

How's that?

Different ways of looking at life rise to the observable surface at times of crisis, threat or change. The conscious search for causes and solutions to an immediate problem reveals much about who we are. We ask, 'What is going on?' from within our particular assumptions about what could be going on. We search along known paths to explain the as yet inexplicable. Causes or solutions that mesh with our view of reality will be accepted as plausible. Others will be rejected.

Let us suppose...

Two strangers come into town one day and end up chatting with a sick man at the outpatients department of the local hospital. The sick man is well known around town; he has a chronic problem thought to be the result of some childhood disease. No one in the community has known him any differently: he has always been a cripple. Later that evening the same man is said to be dancing around the streets of the town, shouting his head off because his lame leg has mended completely. He attributes his cure to the two strangers and, by the way, he doesn't intend to spend any more time in long queues at the hospital!

How would our Western culture generally handle that kind of suggested case history? We have to say first that our culture is extremely sceptical of such an occurrence taking place, full stop! 'Case history' is probably too strong a description of the reported incident; we would feel happier with 'rumour'. If we were to concede that a definite change for the better had taken place in the man's physical condition, we might well use words like 'remission' or 'temporary improvement' or 'time will tell'. Pressed harder we might acknowledge the possibility that the visitors were jolly good psychologists who had helped this sick man overcome the debilitating effects of his lengthy illness, a one in a million chance!

Now let the town be situated far away from the Western world, in another culture. That other culture has no problem acknowledging the 'fact' of the alleged change in the man's condition. That other culture, however, has no concept of 'psychologists' or 'chance'. It therefore concludes very differently. In that culture, no mere human being could perform such a feat on a man diseased in such a way, full stop! To converse with a cripple and see him cured? Only gods can act like that! Therefore the two visitors have to be gods. Gods have been known to come to earth before to intervene in various situations, including that people's national history. The information about such previous visitations has been handed down from generation to generation. Many witnesses attest to other interventions by the gods in human affairs. Now they have come again. These visitors should be offered worship!

Western culture says 'maybe', and if so, then by mind over matter, a rare coincidence. The other culture says 'yes, definitely', not by man or fate but by gods in human form. Both explanations arise from prepackaged ways of looking at life.

Our supposed incident is not completely fictitious. It is a paraphrased retelling of Acts 14:8-18. The place is Lystra, the two visitors are Paul and Barnabas and the sick man is a cripple who has been lame from birth. The purported explanation of the Bible, however, fits neither the Western nor the other cultural context neatly. There is no doubt that the man is instantly healed at Paul's hands: this healing is no rumour! But the apostolic explanation is not couched in terms of remission, chance, psychology or metamorphosed gods, although the last suggestion is noisily put forward by the people of Lystra. The explanation given by the protagonists has to do with faith (v 9) and the bringing of good news from the living God (v 15).

The different cultures 'saw' the situation very differently.

There are approximations to the truth in both the Western and the Lystran explanations of what happened. The Western culture sifts for 'facts' and does eventually concede some kind of change for whatever unknown, but definitely researchable, cause. The Lystran culture easily accepts the changed man but looks in false directions for the explanation, latching on to a fabrication as the real cause. The Scripture states the fact and the true cause, challenging the norms or deep assumptions of Westerner and Lystran alike.

What's it all about?

How we look out on the world may be referred to as our 'worldview'. The processes of that looking out are by and large unconscious. We have all learned to wear our own culture's spectacles without knowing we are doing so, just as we have learned to breathe and sweat and balance without conscious effort. We have gradually emerged an 'Arab' or a 'Briton' or a 'Lystran'.

Worldviews cohere around attitudes or assumptions. They are shared by all, more rather than less, in a particular culture. They enable us to know who we are and how we fit into the world. They furnish us with basic concepts about life, describing what the world is all about, what everything ultimately means. They also tell us what are the norms of life and behaviour, guiding us to act and respond in appropriate ways.

If deep down our worldview tells us that the world is a living organism to be valued and cherished, our cultural conditioning will require us to live in harmony with the world, listening to it, interacting with it, treating it with respect. If deep down our worldview tells us that the world is essentially a neutral 'thing', our cultural conditioning will allow us to subjugate that world, to use it, even abuse it, to live apart from it and to treat it as an 'it'.

If deep down our worldview tells us that the world is full

of invisible spirit beings as well as visible material beings, our cultural conditioning will teach us to live in harmony with those spirit beings as much as with the material beings. If deep down our worldview tells us that only that which is empirical (observable and measurable) is real, we will not be unduly worried about having no concern in our everyday living for 'mythical' spirit beings such as angels or a personal devil.

A model approach

A people's worldview touches everything. All areas of life are impregnated with the meaning given to them by that worldview. The norms of behaviour in those various areas of life reflect that deeper meaning. The kind of structure given to family relationships, for example, depends upon what the worldview says is 'the family': nuclear or extended, patriarchal or matriarchal, monogamous, bigamous or polygamous, age-oriented or youth-oriented, urging equality of the sexes or differentiation of the sexes.

The surface customs of a culture are on show to all observers. In them are expressed the outworkings of the deep-seated assumptions held at worldview level. Figure 2 offers a model of this interrelationship. The differentiated customs in the various areas of life each reflect the underlying worldview of a people. Illustrated here are some customs arising from two different worldviews.

How a culture handles the education of its children, for example, is determined by the norms it holds dear. Do parents want their children to follow in their own footsteps, learning a trade, upholding their function in the clan or tribe? On-the-job or rote learning produces the best results for that end. Do parents want their children to grapple with wider issues or pioneer in academic areas uncharted by themselves? The inductive method of learning best suits this more open-ended objective.

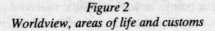

Figure 2
Worldview, areas of life and customs

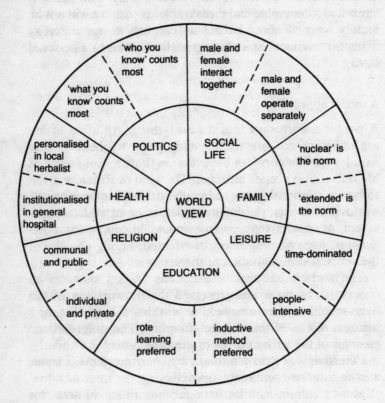

Innermost circle:	underlying worldview of culture
Middle circle:	variety of areas of life in which customs reflect worldview
Outer circle:	examples of different customs reflecting different worldviews

Again, politics may be the province of those who have become expert in different fields of life. A brilliant economist may earn the respect to be nominated as Chancellor of the Exchequer. On the other hand, politics may be the reserve of those who have the good fortune to know the 'right' people. So the relative of a ruler may be appointed to significant national office irrespective of whether he is an expert in that particular field or not! In such a situation loyalty is being valued more highly than expertise.

In all areas of life, the surface customs reflect and contribute to the view of the world which is at the heart of a particular culture.[2]

Collision course

Different ways of looking at life do not come to the observable surface just at times of internal crisis, as in the healing at Lystra. They also appear unmasked when people from different cultures meet or, more often, collide.

One massive collision of cultures over the last twenty years (from the oil crisis in the early 1970s onwards) has occurred between Westerners and Muslim 'fundamentalists'. It is a collision documented in oil-price hikes, wars and rumours of war, ineffective diplomacy, hostage-taking, racism, book-burning and messages in graffiti.

Collisions and their aftermath are uncomfortable! Maybe they cannot be completely avoided. But can their negative effects be minimised? Is there any possibility of standing back from the shock waves to try to understand something of the nature of this particular collision?

The following chapters suggest that there are some steps to be made towards a more healthy understanding of the processes alive in 'West meets East' today.

It is in terms of the worldview model that we propose to offer some 'insider' understanding of Islamic 'fundamentalism'. Our intention is to discover the 'world' which makes sense to the Islamic 'fundamentalist'. Why does he look out upon the world in the way he does? How has his looking thus come about?

Our approach will inevitably pose some questions of the investigator also. What might we learn about ourselves, about our own Western worldview, as a result of exposure to a radically different way of perceiving life? Are there ways in which we can discern the voice of God to us in the fall-out from this competition of worldview?

As we look back upon recent history, upon the story of two different views of the world, is there a way in which, with Christ's help, we can begin to say 'I'm sorry, I'll read that again'?

CHAPTER TWO

PEOPLE WHO LIVE IN GLASS HOUSES SHOULDN'T...

Nice or nasty?

IS HUMAN NAKEDNESS IN PUBLIC NICE, nasty or neutral? The question forced itself upon me in the hills above Santa Barbara, USA, and on the beach at Ayia Napa, Cyprus. It had never really arisen in England—something to do with the weather?

One weekend in the late 1970s, I took a break from studying books at Fuller Theological Seminary in Los Angeles. I journeyed north to visit an American friend living in Santa Barbara. On the hot Saturday afternoon we climbed away from the sticky Pacific heat up into the hills above the coast. We were following the course of a stream.

As we rounded a bend in the path my eyes nearly popped out of my head. Close alongside the path the stream widened and formed pools bounded by large rocks. On these rocks lounged some couples while others were paddling in the pools. The men and women were all completely naked! It dawned on me that these were the only live, mature people, apart from family members, whom I had seen naked. I didn't know where to look as we walked past and on up the path. My friend never batted an eyelid. For him that scene was part of the Californian 'norm'; for me it was shocking.

Soon, however, the shoe was on the other foot. My family had just moved from Egypt to Cyprus when I made the trip to California. We stayed on that beautiful but sadly divided island for two years. An ever-growing tourist industry mushroomed around the seaside resorts of the Greek part of the division. After a couple of summers we had grown quite used to the topless Scandinavians on the sunny southern beaches. Most Cypriot parents, however, found it very difficult coming to terms with such public nakedness and its moral implications for their sons.

What is 'normal' and what becomes 'normal' has to do with worldview and worldview change. The same set of circumstances may be looked upon very differently by people coming to it from different backgrounds.

Is Islamic 'fundamentalism' nice, nasty or neutral? 'Fundamentalism' is one of a number of words used by Westerners to define a movement strongly visible in many Muslim communities around today's world. The people involved in that movement are said to be 'extremist', 'radical' or 'militant' Muslims. Each descriptive term has predominantly negative overtones in Western minds.

Muslims themselves speak just as strongly about that same movement, but the words they use are different. They talk of 'revival', 'renewal', 'resurgence'; words which have, for them, very positive overtones.

The difference in the words used, and the opposite feelings which those words evoke, depict the collision taking place as two radically different views of reality meet each other. As such they well illustrate the model of worldview proposed in Chapter One. In the paragraphs that follow we will try to stand back from the collision and analyse some of the deeper currents at work in this tussle of worldviews.

'Simon says...'

In our Western view of the world, the prevailing 'norm' is secular humanism. Man rules; he decides his own destiny, he lives with the consequences of his failure to manage himself or his world aright. Moreover, it is secular man who rules. There is no more to him than meets the eye. He is not inherently religious. A small minority of individuals may choose to be religious; that is their right. Whatever religious choice they make is also their right: to be a Christian or Taoist or Muslim or whatever. The working hypothesis of Western culture is, however, that man is not intrinsically a religious being. He is a secular being and lives in a secular society.

In the perspective of a 'fundamentalist' Muslim, man is a very different kind of creature. First and foremost he is a creature, created from a clot of blood. He is incurably religious. He is, in fact, Muslim (literally 'submitted to God') by intention. Received, religious values give him direction and guidance in all matters to do with life and living. There is no private area of a person's existence out of which he can lock God: God has a hand in everything.

Western individualism counts for a lot! The role of authority in society is basically to protect individuals' rights. Personal morals and public ethics may be of virtually any variety so long as they do not impose negatively on others' basic human rights. The 'freedom' of the individual to live according to the norms he chooses is paramount.

I well remember a pastoral situation in the Middle East in which I had several verbal skirmishes with a local United States Consul. An American woman, who was also a member of our church, was considerably disturbed and proving very difficult to help. Out of desperation I asked the Consul to arrange for the person to be repatriated before she seriously injured herself. The Consul quoted the 'fifth amendment' as her pretext for doing nothing to help.[3] An American in authority is not allowed to impose on another

American's freedom until or unless some act of aggression has taken place. We had to wait for our friend to damage herself or someone else. 'Freedom' to go too far is part of our Western worldview.

'God' counts for a lot in the view of the Islamic reformist. One such popular visionary, strongly influential in the lead-up to the Iranian revolution, wrote an essay describing how he looked out on the world. He began his first paragraph with the words: 'My worldview consists of *tawḥîd*' (loosely translated 'oneness').[4] The unity of who God is overarches everything. You cannot separate mankind and nature from him. You cannot separate the sacred from the secular and say that mankind has a choice about being religious or not. You cannot hive off 'the religious' from the arena of public life. You cannot break up the 'oneness' of everything in witnessing that there is no god but God.

Rather, you have to say that God has to do with every-thing and has an opinion about everything. That opinion God has made known in different ages to different peoples through the prophets, all agreeing in their messages. In a final sense God has spoken through the Prophet Muham-mad. The true Muslim is the person who in everything is fully submitted to God's perspective. That perspective and the kind of submission expected is revealed through the Qur'ân (supremely) and the example (*sunna*) of the Prophet. Just as all Muslims turn towards the Meccan *kaʿba* to pray, so the worldview of *tawḥîd* demands a turning towards God in all aspects of living.

Who rules OK?

In the collision of worldview that we are examining, the contestants differ markedly from one another. Figures 3 and 4 illustrate, in rather generalised terms, the essence of those differences. Two prevailing dogmas oppose one another: that of secular humanism and that of the doctrine of *tawḥîd*.

On the one hand is Western man, basically a humanist for whom individualism reigns supreme. His world is a secular world, though there is room within it for an individual to hold to some private faith. However, he is not to impose any such faith on others, especially if he is a teacher of religious education in a state school! Basic human rights are the bottom line, while the observable world is his habitat.

On the other hand is the Islamic reformist, a person who sees God as supreme and central to all life. For him, the world is a religious place, man is a religious being, and the main motivation in living is to discern God's will and requirements. God exists and has a view in all the arenas of public and family existence. It becomes a question of submitting or not to that view.

In the eye of the beholder

When Westerners see 'fanatical' Muslim 'extremists' encouraging their young sons to attend their own funerals in mass services before going off to a war front to die, they say, 'This is obscene!' How can Iranian parents send their children to die in Iraqi minefields in a human suicide wave, preparing the way for the regular soldiers? It offends one of the basic values arising from the Western worldview, the value of the individual's right to life.

When reformist Muslims see the Western marital model of sequential polygamy (marriage/divorce/remarriage), they say, 'This is obscene!' How can American parents yield to their children's decisions at eighteen years of age about a marriage partner without any family consultation? It offends one of the basic values arising from the Muslim's worldview, the value of the family's honour, the concern for not bringing shame on the household of God.

When Westerners hear reports of imprisonment or flogging for consumption of alcohol in Muslim countries, they say, 'This is barbaric!' It offends their sense of human equality,

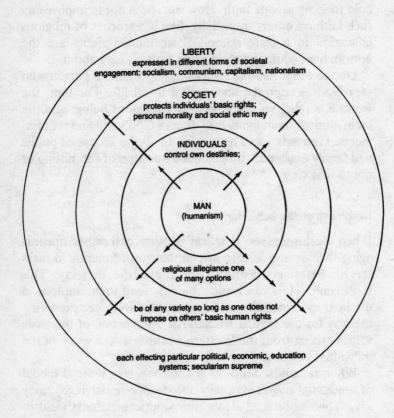

LIBERTY
expressed in different forms of societal
engagement: socialism, communism, capitalism, nationalism

SOCIETY
protects individuals' basic rights;
personal morality and social ethic may

INDIVIDUALS
control own destinies;

MAN
(humanism)

religious allegiance one
of many options

be of any variety so long as one does not
impose on others' basic human rights

each effecting particular political, economic, education
systems; secularism supreme

Figure 3
Worldview of Western secular humanist

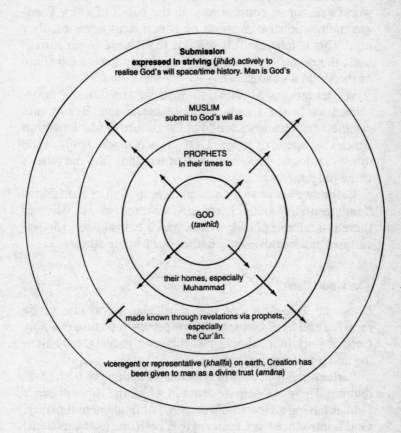

Submission
expressed in striving (jihâd) actively to
realise God's will space/time history. Man is God's

MUSLIM
submit to God's will as

PROPHETS
in their times to

GOD
(tawhîd)

their homes, especially
Muhammad

made known through revelations via prophets,
especially
the Qur'ân.

viceregent or representative (khalîfa) on earth, Creation has
been given to man as a divine trust (amâna)

Figure 4
Worldview of Islamic reformist visionary

the freedom of choice for the individual to be 'wet' or 'dry' within the privacy of his own home.

When reformist Muslims see the control of so much of the world's resources concentrated in the hands of a few Western multinational companies or government agencies, they say, 'This is inhuman!' It offends their sense of creatureliness, the necessity for all human beings to have a fair share of the world's wealth.

Westerners and Muslim reformists hold up differing measuring rods to the society they are evaluating. Beauty and symmetry is, of course, found in the culture or ideology from which they speak or judge. Ugliness is embodied only in the other's customs, the other's way of handling life, the other's value judgements.

Before we move to a detailed examination of the Islamic 'fundamentalist' outlook on life, we need to ask whether there is a reliable platform from which to evaluate societies, cultures and worldviews, whether our own or others.

The Good Book?

Does the Bible present one particular worldview to be received and lived up to, or does it present a picture of a holy Lord at work in a variety of worldviews, judging, enlightening and transforming them?

Perhaps the true answer contains something of both possibilities. There is a definite sense in which the Bible presents God as having a view (the true view) of fundamental reality. God is introduced as Creator. He is both one (self-sufficient) and involved in his creation. The biblical world is a theistic world where God interrelates with the world he has brought into being. It is not a deistic world, in which God sets the universe going and then retires, leaving it to work its own way with no interference from him.

In the biblical world, the God who is absolute and beyond cultural limitation displays his hand, as it were, and makes known certain unchangeable things. His opinion is the true opinion: the world and mankind is created, not eternal; man is innately a religious being; there will be consistency in the created world until the time of judgement; Jesus Christ is the Saviour and Lord of all.

Certain values follow from such fundamentals and those are enshrined in stone in the Old Testament Decalogue and on the hearts of the remnant after the exile to Babylon. Some norms are presented in the New Testament as absolute. Oneness in Christ, for example, overrides claims of being firstly male or female, Jew or Gentile, slave or freeman.

So there are elements of supracultural truth which impinge, through the pages of Scripture, on all mankind.

There is also a definite sense in which the Bible presents God as exquisitely satisfied with a variety of culture-bound responses to him. As we shall reflect in the final chapters of this book, the movement of salvation history is towards an occasion when those from each tribe and tongue and nation shall offer their worship to the Lamb. The momentum of divine revelation is that of incarnation, away from centralisation and blueprint towards the risk of the eternal Word becoming human and being misunderstood.

So Jews can become true Jews in knowing their Messiah, while Gentiles can become disciples of the Way without having to become Jews first. Jesus can ask his penetrating questions in Aramaic, have them recorded in common Greek and still speak through them to Russian, Chinese and Brazilian hearts, centuries later.

While some biblical norms come across as absolute, others appear to be local and negotiable in the transforming of specific attitudes in particular cultural settings. In terms of the offering of Christian worship, for example, synagogue gatherings largely give way to house worship, and Sabbath gatherings yield to Lord's Day meetings as the Book of Acts proceeds.

God's line in the sand

Where is the supracultural God saying that a certain, absolute perspective is essential for all mankind? Where is he saying that what already exists is lovely and expresses his life? Where is he saying that what already exists is an acceptable starting point but needs transforming by the light of Christ?

I am an Anglican vicar and at the moment one big debate in the Church of England is about the ordination of women to the priesthood. Those in favour of such ordination tend to argue that women 'priests' are a culturally appropriate expression of ministry in the Western church today. Those against such ordination often maintain that the all-male pattern set by Jesus in his ministry is a supracultural revelation by God to be adhered to faithfully for ever in all cultural settings.

The Anglican debate is mirrored in other denominations over issues of authority and pastoral practice, such as the type of baptism, eldership, Bible translation, public prayer, dress which is 'scriptural'. The vigour with which we all argue our case marks our concern to be faithful to Scripture. But where does the divine desire for uniformity end and the divine delight in unity-in-diversity begin? Are we all so sure that in our own particular constellation of interpretations it is God, not us, who is drawing the line?

I have a feeling that there are other, far more fundamental issues that God is concerned about for Western Christians, Anglicans included. Those issues have to do with our basic outlook on life as Westerners. They don't really come up for question (unlike issues of church order) because we all implicitly agree about them.

Why have we denigrated to an area of private opinion matters which in both Old Testament and New were deemed public: the fact that we are created, the fact that our world is a spiritual battleground, the fact that gospel-sharing has to be as much 'in deed' as in word, the fact that man is a spiritual as well as a material being, the fact that the world belongs to God and we only tenant it? In many of these basic areas, the irony of the situation is that modern Islamic 'fundamentalists' adhere to a worldview far closer to the biblical norm than our Western aberration.

Of course, there are equally fundamental blind spots in the reformist Muslim's outlook on life. The Bible poses different questions to that worldview. What kind of God is the human image reflecting where rulership is the bottom line? According to the reformists, man is God's viceregent on earth. How would the God of resurgent Islam have man sort out the created world? The model for believers is the Medinan rulership of Muhammad: sword as well as word. Justice easily takes on the bad taste of mercilessness, of revenge murders on a massive scale, of raw pride when suffering for righteousness' sake is not part of the divine nature of things. No reformist Muslim leader can stop an aircraft hijacking or a Kurdish genocide and say, 'This is contrary to God's nature.' No reformist Muslim can freely pursue a reconciliatory role, calling the faithful and the faithless to forgive one another: the victory of God's party, not mutual forgiveness, is the point. No reformist Muslim can propose a solution in terms of sinful men being made 'new creations' for he believes ultimately that man is not a sinner, just weak: that is how God made him.

Fundamental issues about who man is have massive repercussions in a worldview which purports to carry sanction from the ultimate source for every powerful act, in public and in private. Life has to be lived in a certain manner because God himself says so.

We will return to this interrogation of 'Western' and 'fundamentalist' worldviews in our closing chapters. Meanwhile we need to look more closely at the manifesto of the reformist ideologists. What are they 'for', and what are they 'against'?

CHAPTER THREE

ROADSIDE HARVEST!

I T SEEMED SO LONG SINCE SALAH AL-DIN had last gazed at that late-summer patchwork of browns and reds, beiges and yellows. From his childhood, he had grown to anticipate those great annual squares of fruity colour carpeting the roadside dust outside his village, north of Kabul. The massive transformation of grape to raisin took time under the trees' shade. The slowed rhythm became a seasonal pause after the heat of picking, when both fruit and man seemed to mature, change and take stock for winter.

The pretty picture flickered in the guerilla's mind as Salah al-Din returned to the unlovely present. The patch of drying grapes hardened and focused. Grenades! Lying at his feet, carefully laid with pins accessible to his left hand, ready for grabbing with his right, this modern Afghan fruit seemed so impersonal, so unnatural. These were the hard implements of human harvesting. What had his country come to that grenades had to carpet his native soil, awaiting his tug and throw?

Salah al-Din shifted weight carelessly, kicking the gravel in the bottom of the drainage channel beside the road. He glanced to his right, taking in the nervous preparations of his fellow mujahideen. A small bank on the road side of the drainage channel separated the string of turbaned guerillas from the noisy tanks crashing along the highway a few metres away.

'Eighteen, nineteen, twenty,' he counted as the heavy caterpillar tracks vibrated the ground and loosened the soil in the drainage channel. Small avalanches of dust rivuleted down around Salah al-Din's feet. He picked up a grenade, tossed it from one hand to another and kissed it.

'I hate you,' he whispered to it, 'but I hate them more! You must speak for my father, and my father's brother and his family.' His knuckles shone white as he squeezed the hard casing. 'How dare they! God damn them! Infidels!'

Breathing deeply with deliberation, Salah al-Din checked his passion. Self-control gradually returned to the sensitive man. 'O God, please take away the haunting nightmare about that violent evening in my clan village! It's the thought of what they must have gone through before death brought its merciful release. That's what I cannot bear! That's what I can never forgive! Let these grenades declare my anger.'

Salah al-Din concentrated on the cold formalities of modern revenge-taking. His right hand caressed the surface of the grenade, gently selecting the ridges and indentations, finding the best grip for a firm throw.

A movement up the ditch, some 200 metres, caught his eye—the first signal. Salah al-Din braced himself, listening carefully now. A tank was slightly to his right, drawing level. He imagined the distance, the angle, the look of surprise from the commander in the turret should he chance to see his left bank spring to turbaned life, the curving flight, the streak of magnesium white, the report, the pitch of the tank, and then the inferno, the noise, the screams, the screams.

'God guide my arm,' he hissed, fingers of his left hand closing on the pin, ready to pull, feet shifting again, stabilising his crouched body, ready to spring. 'God, guide us all. Let it be the battle of Badr again and again!'

A green turban flashed to the ground. Salah al-Din and twenty other mujahideen became instant silhouettes, flashing shadows on the bank of a road in northern Afghanistan. Unisoned arks of explosive vengeance curled outward and over the unsuspecting Russian tanks.

Stone-hard grapes of wrath winged towards another bloody toll.

CHAPTER FOUR

PARADISE LOST?

Fundamentally against

IT IS DIFFICULT TO EXTRACT A PRECISE DEFINI-
TION of the Islamic reformists' goals, for they differ in
various parts of the world. The mujahideen of
Afghanistan seek the complete 'liberation' of their homeland. They may have banished the tanks, but their continuing objective is Islam in place of Russian political or
economic imperialism. The National Salvation (*Milli
Selamet*) Party of Turkey wants a reversal of the deliberate
secularisation of that country. The Islamic Organisation
(*Jamâ'at-i Islâmî*) of Pakistan desires a government that will
wholeheartedly introduce Islamic law as the sole basis of
jurisprudence there.

Perhaps the common denominator in the expression of
Islamic reformist movements is that they are all 'against'
something or someone. They are against the 'Great Satan'—
the USA, against Mrs Thatcher, against President Mubarak
of Egypt or King Fahd of Saudi Arabia. They are against the
State of Israel, against dependence upon the West, against
usury. They are against both-sex physical education lessons,
against Salman Rushdie, against the Aḥmadîyas, against
saints and shrines and Sufis.

Against them make ready
Your strength to the utmost
Of your power, including
Steeds of war, to strike terror
Into (the hearts of) the enemies... (sura 8:60).

The proof text for many Islamic reformists is supplied in this verse of the Qur'ân. Indeed, its first word appears in Arabic on the logo of the Muslim Brotherhood.[5]

The distinguished philosopher and poet, Sir Muḥammad Iqbâl, inspired millions of his fellow Muslims in India to fight for self-reform and self-realisation as part of a movement towards independent nationhood after British colonial rule. He expresses a similar sentiment in verse:

Against Europe I protest
And the attraction of the West:
Woe for Europe and her charm,
Swift to capture and disarm!
Europe's hordes with flame and fire
Desolate the world entire;
Architect of Sanctuaries,
Earth awaits rebuilding; rise!
Out of leaden sleep,
Out of slumber deep
    Arise!
Out of slumber deep
    Arise![6]

There is a certain general agreement concerning the 'against' programme of reformist Islam, particularised in different countries and historic periods. Muslim revivalists are against what they feel is imposed upon them and which is false to their view of faithfulness to God.

Perhaps most of the 'against' shouting appearing on our television screens seems to be directed against foreigners. At times this has certainly been reflective of the truth. Westerners have been the butt of effigy-burning and public demonstration by Muslims. For the most part, however, reformist Muslims are expressing an anxiety about the world of the 'believers'. Their intended audience is their own people. The status quo in contemporary Muslim societies is what piques them most. In their view, that status quo is unacceptable and they want to see it changed.

Fundamentally for

Stated positively, the goal of Muslim reformists is the renewal of society in all its aspects. They promote revival (*tajdîd*) or reform (*islâh*). Their concern about the state of the 'house of Islam' is not particularly new, although it may be something that seems new to non-Muslim onlookers. Most reformists see themselves as part of a continuing revivalist tradition in Islamic history.

Central to that tradition is the call for a return to the fundamentals of Islam. To be a Muslim today, in the reformists' view, should amount to living in an Islamic state, being governed by Islamic law, and pursuing a heaven-inspired mission in the world. Most reformist movements, therefore, have as a major demand or objective the proper establishment in their country of an Islamic state.

Religion and politics

In order to investigate the Muslim reformist's concern for the establishment of an Islamic state, an overtly political goal, we need to return to our model of worldview. As that model applies to the Islamist's outlook on life, we discover that God and a sense of *tawhîd* (oneness or holism) are pivotal in his view of the world. Such acknowledgement of the divine's core involvement in human life ripples out into all areas of perceiving and living. Religion is intimately connected with politics, law, family life, customs, commerce, and so on. God has a view on everything. There is a divine attitude to be discerned and put into effect. The worldview finds its authenticity in being theocratic, totally God-centred. The Muslim's obligation as submitted creature and upright viceregent (God's deputy) is to realise God's will in history. That obligation is communal as much as individual. It touches everyone and everything.

The focus of the working out of that obligation is the Islamic state. It is in the Islamic state that true 'submission' (*islâm*) finds proper expression. Such a state comprises a community of believers. God is the ultimate sovereign, his law is the basis for societal interaction, and religious scholars are the guardians of the tradition. The legitimacy of a Muslim government is measured by the ruler's commitment to upholding Islamic (*sharî a*) law.

Figure 5 expresses the interrelationship of the major components of the Islamic state. Community, law and leadership, given and guided by God himself, is the major premise and objective in such a society. Religion and politics go hand in hand in reformist Islam.

As it was in the beginning

'Back to the good old days' is not wholly wistful thinking for Muslims. The Medinan period under the caliphate of Muhammad himself is recalled with warmth and pride. Those were the formative years in which the Prophet and his Companions learned what it meant to live under the sovereignty of God. They had withdrawn from Mecca, shaking the dust from their sandals at the people's unbelief. In Medina, Muhammad gradually structured a society based on 'the Word of the Lord'.

The belief of those early Muslims in the divinely ordained nature and objectives of the Medinan community was strengthened by the successes of that period. After all, if God is the overall sovereign, shouldn't one expect considerable success?

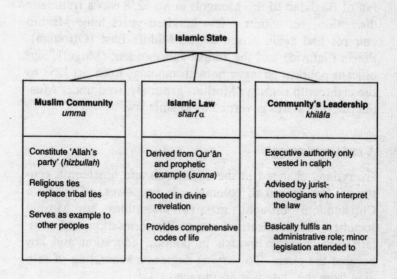

Figure 5
Components of the Islamic state

The same kind of validation of the Muslim community continued to be expected and experienced after Muhammad's death. Political domination affirmed that the submission was proper, pleasing to God. Within a hundred years the Islamic community had become one of the largest imperial expanses ever known. Geographically vast, the Muslim world also spawned major contributions to philosophy, mathematics, geometry, optics, the physical sciences and the arts.

In subsequent history, despite several major setbacks, Islamic reformists still discern strong traces of the working out of the divine intention down through the centuries. The fall of Baghdad to the Mongols in AD 1258 was a traumatic disruption, yet within a few hundred years huge Muslim empires had again arisen in the Middle East (Ottoman), Persia (Safavid) and the Indian subcontinent (Mogul). Significant political changes notwithstanding, from AD 1258 to the eighteenth century, Muslims generally lived under Muslim rulers in states governed by Islamic law.

A rude awakening!

Everything changed in the eighteenth and nineteenth centuries! The spread of colonial rule by powers of Western Christendom brought massive alterations to Muslim societies. 'Modernisation' meant Westernisation and secularisation. Foreign models in politics, education and law became the norm. To varying degrees a separating of religion from the state was encouraged.

Western constitutions and legal codes remained the norm as eventual preparations were made towards the granting of independence. A Western worldview was superimposed on the indigenous one. Western educated and Westernised élites were prepared to manage the emerging, independent, twentieth-century states. In Muslim countries the prevailing religio-political expression of Islam was strongly eclipsed.

The everyday realities of colonial rule were focused in the restructuring of the political processes to constitute a secular state. The imposition by force of this Western political model upon Muslim societies in the Middle East and beyond was bound to produce huge shock waves, for the Islamic state and the secular state are like chalk and cheese. They are incompatible, arising from different views of what life is all about.

'Human' or 'divine'?

Figure 6 contrasts two approaches to communal, political life: the Islamic state and the secular state. One approach arises out of an Islamic 'fundamentalist' worldview, the other out of a fundamentally secularist worldview. One openly declares that it is revealed by God, the other equally strongly avows that it is born of human reason.

The points of differentiation are many. There can be no legislation independent of God's will in an Islamic state. There can be no legislation sanctioned purely on religious grounds in a secular state.

An Islamic state is an ideological state; it is the commonness of ideological commitment which marks it as distinct from other human communities. A secular state is a national state; it is the commonness of locality which distinguishes it from other states.

An Islamic state has to be controlled and run exclusively by Muslims, people committed to the ideology for which it exists. A secular state can be controlled and run by representative individuals of any religious or ethnic persuasion so long as they are true citizens of that nation.

In an Islamic state, the legislative function of government is a given. God has revealed the law in the Qur'ân and the example (*sunna*) of the Prophet. What is needed is a right administration of that legislation. Perhaps in minor matters, details of law-making need some enacting, but the major functions of government are to provide executive and judicial skills. A secular state flourishes only with the independent functioning of the legislature, the executive and the judiciary.

Religion enters every detail of public life in an Islamic state. God has something to say on every matter. In public health or education, being Muslim is part of the job: norms revealed in Qur'ân and *sunna* guide policy decisions. In the

Islamic State	Secular State
Governed in accordance with the laws of God as revealed in Qur'ân and *sunna*	Governed by laws made through human reason
Ultimate sovereignty belongs only to God	The state must itself be fully sovereign
Umma comprises the community of the faithful; allegiances reach beyond national barriers	The state must be national; individuals' allegiance is to the nation
Aspires to become a universal state	The state must have a well-defined territory
Executive and judicial authorities alone are required; some minor matters justify legislature	Requires legislative, executive and judicial authorities
Guarantees the rights of all citizens but some hold only *dhimmî* (non-Muslim minority) status	All citizens are equal before the law
All public life is religious	Religion is part of the private domain
Modelled on Muhammad's leadership in Medina	Modelled (originally) on the Greek concept of nation-state

Figure 6
The Islamic state and the secular state

secular state, religion is part of the private domain. Teachers, government ministers, judges and doctors can all decide whether or not they believe in God. Their believing or not has nothing to do with their public duties in which they are engaged.

Two views of life, of political process, of 'religion' are thus strongly opposed. The traditional Islamic model was eclipsed in a way never previously experienced when the European powers colonised the non-Western world. 'Paradise' was suddenly and drastically lost.

The new colonial or protectorate rules challenged the very meaning of Muslim history. What did the success of 'infidel' armies indicate? What did the rapid enslavement of Muslim communities to foreign economic and political systems say about God's sovereignty? What had gone wrong with Islam?

And how were things to be rectified? In the moves towards independence, many Muslims would find fuel for anti-colonialist slogans and activities in a renewed emphasis upon 'Islam'. Reformist Muslims, among others, would contribute their energies towards the regaining of a lost 'paradise'. How well did they do?

To the processes of independence-seeking and the question of its success in reinstating an 'Islam' espoused by the reformists, we now turn.

CHAPTER FIVE

OUT OF THE FRYING PAN...

The ugly European

A FEW YEARS AT THE END OF THE NINETEENTH CENTURY saw the consolidation of strong control by Britain over old and new colonies. In 1875, Prime Minister Disraeli bought a controlling interest in the Suez Canal from Egypt's ruler. In 1876, Queen Victoria was declared Empress of India. At the Congress of Berlin in 1878, Disraeli won Cyprus for Britain. British imperialism was at its height. A typical Western encyclopedia summarises quite simply: 'British people of all classes watched proudly as Britain expanded its influence in China, the Middle East, and Africa.'[7]

What was true for Britain was also true for Spain, Portugal, the Netherlands, France, Italy, Belgium, Germany and Russia. Prior to 1945, more than 99 per cent of the non-Western world was under Western domination.

From the perspective of Muslims in that non-Western world, the European colonial domination was cause for great shame. Militarily, economically and eventually politically, the Muslim world succumbed to the powers of what was Western Christendom. The essential meaning of Muslim history was up for question. What had gone so wrong as to cause this international state of affairs?

The widespread disintegration of the traditional Islamic political order and the struggle against European colonialism provided not only an identity crisis for Muslims but also a political purpose. The crushing culminated in an eventual resurrection.

During the twentieth century, 'Islam' re-emerged strongly in the politics of the Muslim world. Appeal to fellow countrymen on the basis of their being Muslims inspired anti-colonial, nationalist movements. Religion gave cohesion to struggles for independence in many Muslim countries.

Voices in the wilderness

Jamâl al-Dîn al-Afghânî (1839–1897) was an early, lone voice in demanding an end to the rule of Britannia. He was reputedly born in Afghanistan but moved to India while still young. There he grew to hate the imperialism of the British. The expression of that hatred led to his being successively expelled from Afghanistan, Turkey and Egypt. His provocative thoughts remained long after his expulsions, however, and had strong effect on some men in Egypt and Syria especially. Afghani called upon Muslims to resist imperialism, to pursue political liberation and to seek once again their own identity in a return to pristine Islam.[8]

An Egyptian, Muḥammad ʿAbduh (1849–1905), and a Syrian, Rashîd Riḍâ (1865–1935), agreed with Afghani's diagnosis of what was wrong and what needed doing. They began a movement (the *Salafîya*) with its own journal (*al-Manar*) which carried the ideas of Afghani throughout the Muslim world from North Africa to Southeast Asia. Islam became the motivating force and Muslim nationalism the surface expression for a rejection of European colonialism and a struggle for independence.

In North Africa, where there were serious ethnic divisions

between Arabs and Berbers, Islam supplied the common ground for anti-colonial activities.

In the Indian subcontinent, the original Hindu-Muslim independence movement shattered as Muslims sought a different reconstruction of the political world. They wanted something more than minority status in a Hindu world when the British finally left. Under the emerging leadership of Muḥammad Iqbâl (1875–1938) and Muḥammad 'Alî Jinnâḥ (1876–1948) the call for a separate Muslim state became strident.

In Indonesia, Islam provided the foundation and leaders for that country's first mass nationalist movement. The Islamic League (*Sarekat Islam*), founded in 1911, owned Islam as its ideological cornerstone and strove to regroup the Muslim voices spread throughout the Indonesian islands. Indeed, the Islamic League became the very symbol of national aspirations prior to Sukarno's founding (in 1927) of the Indonesian National Party.

Islam played a less significant role in some of the countries of the Middle East due to the presence in Syria, Lebanon and Egypt of an articulate Christian minority. Such Christians helped make the issue less one of Islam versus colonialism and more one of Arab nationalism versus colonialism. Many Christian Syrians, Lebanese, Palestinians and Egyptians spoke as Arabs demanding freedom for Arab nations.

Turning of the tide

For a complex variety of reasons the twenty-five years following World War II saw the rapid demise of political imperialism by the Western powers. By 1965, more than 99 per cent of the non-Western world was independent. Figure 7 describes the extrication of Muslim nations from Western colonial rule or influence.

Period of Independence	Name of Emerging Nation
1943-45	Lebanon, Syria
1946-49	Jordan, Pakistan, (India), Indonesia
1950-55	Libya, Egypt
1956-60	Sudan, Morocco, Tunisia, Malaysia, Somalia, Niger, Chad, Senegal, Mali, Nigeria, Mauretania
1961-65	Kuwait, Algeria, Maldive Islands
1966-69	Southern Yemen

Figure 7
Muslim extrication from Western colonial rule

The foreign masters were gone. Muslims, and others, could again lift their heads high in self-respect. Or could they?

For ever 'England'?

When the French troops left Algeria or the British 'protectorate' in Egypt faded, what emerged in their place? When British India was partitioned and Pakistan born as a separate Muslim nation, how was that new country to operate under Jinnah, its popular Governor General? To what extent did Islam colour the Muslim nations of Syria, Jordan, and Egypt? To what degree did the emerging governments of the newly independent countries return their nations to the 'proper' rule of Islam?

From the Islamic reformist's perspective, the sad truth is that European rule left a lasting legacy on the post-colonial Muslim nations. There was no real move from a subject, secular state to an independent Islamic state. What emerged in country after country was a disappointing hybrid: a cross between a Western secular state and a legitimate Islamic state.

The withdrawal of foreign troops and political power holders did not mean an automatic demise of the institutions previously established under the colonial tutelage. There now existed in many situations two sources of political input. On the one hand was the Western model taken over and somewhat adapted by the emerging leaderships of the newly independent nations. On the other hand was the residual, revived Islamic model, championed by the reformist visionaries and their supporters. Figure 8 illustrates the areas of social life in which conflicting priorities might be expected as alternative models of statehood vie for ascendancy.

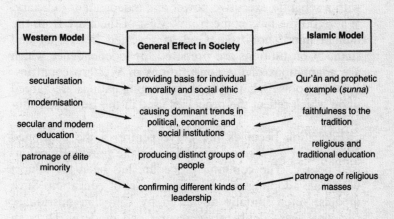

Figure 8
The Western and Islamic reformist models of statehood

Legacy of the West

Secularisation constitutes the biggest heartache for the reformists. Instead of the Qur'ân and prophetic example (*sunna*) being the only sources for public and private standards of ethic, secularisation introduces an altogether different element. Secularisation is based upon a humanistic concept of the world. To the secularist, divine guidance is irrelevant. Other motives push the Qur'ân and *sunna* into the background. A rationalist approach suggests that a twentieth-century society is not to be established and maintained on a faith basis. Instead, a capitalist or socialist/communist philosophy provides a better empirical guide to nation-building. Social institutions, inheritance law, the rights of women, health education are all geared to making a secularised vision of society work in the newly 'independent' country.

Modernisation means, in the reformist's view, 'Westification'. Patterns of Western dominance are deeply fixed in the colony's institutional make-up. A legislature is established, with a separate executive power and independent judiciary. Where do the laws come from? Most of them are from the human mind, not from God as revealed in Qur'ân and *sunna*. Constitutions are prepared for independence which are adaptations of the constitutions of Western countries. Forms of power-sharing in the emerging nations are agreed upon which reflect the processes used in the European situation.

Education becomes the nerve centre of the continued imposing of a Western worldview on the previously colonised people. The common procedure has been the almost wholesale adopting of a Western model of education. Such models, often initially advanced by Christian missionary societies, were deliberately secular and modern. Through them the culture and values of the 'teachers' were passed to the indigenous learners. European concepts of 'progress' were imbibed by students of the ruling power.

Recruitment of non-Western nations into the great

Western debate—capitalism versus communism—and the great Western political programme—World War II—epitomises how deeply the colonisers had convinced the colonised of their view of the world. When the Europeans left, the educational structures were taken over by the new ruling élite. In some cases, more traditional Islamic forms of education were upgraded, but by and large the Western approach was positively maintained.

Western patronage during colonial rule produced a national leadership far removed from the traditional ideal of leadership in an Islamic state. Indeed, in many instances the traditional leaders of Muslim society were deliberately compromised and undermined. The normal procedure was for a foreign political leadership to be directly imposed upon the subject peoples, followed by the grooming of a foreign-oriented local leadership. This prepared élite would lead the colonised countries after independence. Such leadership would ensure a continuing recruitment of those nations to the programmes and designs of the retiring imperial powers.

The emerging national leaders quickly grew distant from the mass of their own people, and were increasingly suspected and hated. They have often been the assassination targets of Islamic reform movements seeking full independence from the cultural implications of colonial rule.

Too steep a price?

When Muslim countries won their independence in those twenty-five years after World War II, the societies which emerged constituted a mishmash in the eyes of the Islamic reformists. The people who led the countries to freedom were often personally compromised in their view, part of the foreign-educated élite who would direct the new nation along paths previously learned from foreigners. It was independence à la Western mode.

Two countries were quite deliberately secularised. Turkey

and Iran were to be part of the new world, modern, West-oriented. The bitter pill of the abolition of the caliphate in Turkey emphasised just how awry loyalty to Islam had gone at the beginning of this century. The shift in Iran towards the Pahlavi identification with King Cyrus rather than Prophet Muhammad set the Iranian reformists' teeth on edge. Even a country such as Pakistan, deliberately titled 'The Islamic Republic of Pakistan' within nine years of its creation, was heavily secularised in terms of its institutional and judicial life.

The involvement of Islamic reformists in independence movements must not be misunderstood. They were heavily involved. Their total programme, however, was not shared by the newly emerging political leadership of the nations concerned. The Islamic reformists' intention has consistently been the same: a renewal of society by a return to the pristine, authentic Islam of the Medinan period. In the first part of this century that necessitated a throwing off of the imperial yoke.

Imperialism, however, was but part and parcel of a greater evil in the minds of the Islamic reformists. All that stood in the way of the implementation of Islamic law or the rule of the *Imâm* (in Shî'a society[9]) had to be brought crashing down. It was the worldview motivating the Western colonisers which remained behind after the Europeans left. It is that worldview which is the perpetual enemy. For the Islamic reformists, the worldview of *tawḥîd* has been the constant goal towards which they and all true.Muslims have been moving. Such movement gained considerable momentum during the break from imperialism, but the mere departure of Westerners in no way guaranteed the bringing in of the reformists' vision for a divine order on earth.

Today's pearl in the oyster!

In the post-colonial period, the Islamic reformists believe that they have something authentic to offer the Muslim world. They conceive of themselves as part of a continuous chain of irritants within the house of Islam pleading with the community, the *umma*, to be faithful to the calling of God in Qur'ân and prophetic tradition (*sunna*).

Comprehensive reform, with faith at the centre of all life, is their common demand. Sir Muḥammad Iqbâl and Mawlânâ Sayyid Abû'l-ʿAlâ' Mawdûdî have been at the hub of such demands on the Indian subcontinent. In Egypt, Imâm Ḥasan al-Bannâ' Shahîd and Sayyid Qutb Shahîd were both martyred (*shahîd* means 'martyr' in Arabic) for the reformist cause. Their writings have inspired many contemporary Egyptian reformists. Iranian Muslims have been strongly motivated by the works and speeches of Dr ʿAlî Shari'ati and Imam Khomeini[10] in the years up to and beyond the 1979 revolution. Mâlik bin Nabî and Shaikh Ibraḥîm al-Jazâ'ir in Algeria and Said Nursi in Turkey are other important spokesmen for the reformist view.

In the next section of this book we will look briefly at the histories and writings of some of these men. Their reformist teachings are selectively summarised against the background of their different political contexts. Some of them were proponents of movements towards independence. Others tried to bring a corrective note to newly independent nations which, in their view, were going wrong. In their eyes, it was too often a case of 'Out of the frying pan, into the fire!' Behind the variety will be discovered something of the common worldview out of which such visionaries spoke and acted.

PART 2

CHAPTER SIX

MASTERMIND

Strategy for a General

What is the meaning of Pakistan?
There is no god but one God.[11]

I
T IS THE BIRTHDAY OF THE HOLY PROPHET. The year is 1979. For the first time in Pakistan, many major events are officially organised to celebrate the feast. The country's leader, General Zia ul-Haq, sums up the regime's commitment to a more Islamic way of national life in his slogan concerning the real meaning of Pakistan. He goes on to describe some of the policy details designed to wed a nation to an Islamic ideology.

Two years into his rule, General Zia is putting flesh on the approach he had publicly announced immediately after the coup d'état which brought him to power. With the country under martial law, the General had quickly distanced himself from the deposed Prime Minister Zulfiqar ʿAli Bhutto. The new leader revealed the all-embracing objective for his period of rule: the introduction to the people of Pakistan of an Islamic system of life.[12]

The words were the General's, but the strategy came from another gentleman. That strategy had been expressed quite clearly some thirty years previously in a lecture at the Law College in Lahore:

> I am sure that if a righteous group of people, possessing vision and statesmanship, wields political power and, making full use of the administrative machinery of the government, utilizes all the resources at its disposal for the execution of a well conceived plan of national regeneration, the collective life of this country can be totally changed within a period of ten years.[13]

The gentleman who was so sure back in 1948 was Abûl-'Alâ' Mawdûdî (Mawdudi).

Family background

Mawdudi was born in Hyderabad in 1903. His name derived from Khawajah Qutb al-Dîn Mawdûd, a renowned leader of the Chishti order of Sufis. The saintly forbear had lived in India in the twelfth century.

Mawdudi's father saw to it that his son was instructed in the basics of Islam. He employed tutors to teach the boy Arabic, Persian and Urdu. Only later in life did Mawdudi study English, at a time when his career required knowledge of that language. Mawdudi's father, a barrister by profession, was strongly disillusioned with the British imperial presence in India. Part of his care for his son's education was motivated by his desire to isolate the lad from the influences of European education and culture.

Early career

Mawdudi's father died when he was seventeen. That same year Mawdudi began a career in journalism which was to propel him to the forefront of a growing groundswell of Muslim concern for their future in an India-after-the-British. For ten years Mawdudi edited a variety of newspapers, ending with *al-Jamia*, the daily newspaper of a society of reformist

Muslim scholars (the Association of the Muslim Divines of India, or *Jami'at al-'Ulama-i Hind*). This paper was religiously oriented, strongly anti-British and anti-Hindu. Through his editorship of *al-Jamia*, Mawdudi met many leaders of Indian Muslim thought.

In the early 1930s, Mawdudi shifted from journalism to more literary work, joining and almost immediately taking over a journal called *Exegesis of the Qur'ân* (*Tarjumân al-Qur'ân*). This publication became Mawdudi's mouthpiece for a systematic exposition of an Islamic world order. His purpose was to expose the evil of the modernistic, Western expression of *jâhilîya* (ignorance, faithlessness to God), and to exegete a proper Islamic way of life. *Exegesis of the Qur'ân* also provided Mawdudi with a means for recalling the Indian Muslim leadership especially to such a purified Islam.

Turning points

In 1925 a murder occurred which shook Mawdudi. A Muslim extremist killed a Hindu religious teacher, Swami Shradhanand. Swami Shradhanand had led the *Shuddhi* movement in its efforts to reconvert to Hinduism some of the depressed classes of India who were nominally Muslim. The murder provoked a lot of agitation by Hindus against Muslims. Mawdudi tried to answer criticisms of Islam through the daily paper *al-Jamia*, an effort which consolidated in his own mind what he felt was the Islamic view of life. His editorials were later published as a book on the subject of holy war (*jihâd*).

In 1937 Mawdudi was shaken again. He realised that India, after 150 years of control by the British, was on the brink of independence. His contemporaries, members of many different political perspectives, were all debating the shape of the future India. Muslims throughout the nation were frightened of being swallowed up totally in the civilisation of a Hindu majority. The Indian National Congress, a mainly Hindu party, affirmed that all Indians should in future constitute a single nation under a democratic and secular government. Muslims, led by the Muslim League, went along with the Congress party in its opposition to British rule, but argued the need for separate electorates and constitutional guarantees for autonomous Muslim provinces. The Muslim leaders of this mass political movement, based on Islamic identity, comprised a Western-educated élite. Mawdudi did not trust that élite at all. For four years he wrote constantly on political matters and the implications of contemporary discussions for Muslims.

Mawdudi urged Muslims not to join the freedom struggle led by the Indian National Congress and its nationalist Muslim supporters, headed by Muhammad Ali Jinnah. Positively, though perhaps with his head a little in the clouds, Mawdudi proposed that if Indian Muslims returned to being truly Muslim, they could actually change the whole of India into an Islamic state. If the communist or fascist minorities in Europe could grab and manipulate majorities into their own images, could not faithful Muslims in India expect to dominate the majority in their country—given that they returned first to a pure Islam?

A third shock came to Mawdudi in 1940. The elections of 1937 had resulted in defeat for the Muslim League. After the elections, Congress had refused to share control of the government with Muslim League politicians. The League leaders had reacted by intensifying demands. 'Separate electorates' vaporised in the slipstream of Jinnah's 'two nations' theory. In 1940, the Muslim League published its 'Lahore Resolution' calling for the establishment of separate states in the Muslim majority areas of India. The demand was public and popular for 'Pakistan'. Mawdudi felt strongly that such partition was useless. Along with the Association of Muslim Divines, he opposed the movement for a separate 'nation' for Indian Muslims. Perhaps Mawdudi preferred the devil-he-knew of a united India with safeguards for Muslim law and custom to the devil-unknown of a Jinnah-led, separate Muslim nation? He certainly felt that a separate territory for Muslims would in no way guarantee that they would form an 'Islamic' nation, while the substantial Muslim populations left in India would be viewed with hostility by the majority Hindus.

In 1941 Mawdudi launched his reply to the Lahore Resolution. He invited various interested Muslims to meet him in Lahore where the Islamic Organisation (*Jamâ'at-i Islâmî*) was born, with Mawdudi as its first director. Mawdudi sought an informed and motivated group of Muslim leaders who would train others until the opportunity presented itself of their wielding political power and controlling the administrative machinery and thus establishing an Islamic state. From its foundation in 1941 to the partition of India in 1947, the Islamic Organisation organised and educated. Meanwhile, the Muslim League won an overwhelming victory in the 1945 elections, emerging as the sole representative of Muslim political interests in the subcontinent. The movement towards a separate nation for many of India's Muslims was unstoppable.

Pakistan?

At the time of partition, Mawdudi was living with some of his disciples in community in East Punjab. They called themselves House of Islam (*Dâr al-Islâmî*). The horrors of partition forced the majority of the group to emigrate to Lahore. Mawdudi, who had so strenuously opposed the creation of Pakistan, quickly came to terms with the new reality. Within West Pakistan his society assisted refugees pouring westwards into that half of the infant Muslim homeland.

Politically, the Islamic Organisation launched a campaign calling for an Islamic state in Pakistan. Mawdudi argued that the prime object of the creation of Pakistan was to establish an Islamic state, an entity in which Islamic law (the *shariʿa*) would define the parameters of banking and commerce, of public and private conventions. From 1947 until 1956, when the Pakistan constitution was finally published, Mawdudi and his society fought for an Islamic constitution. Mawdudi's concept of an Islamic state was of a strongly centralised structure, run on authoritarian lines with the help of a strong army.

Members of the Islamic Organisation played their part in the marginalising of the Aḥmadîya community and made their provocative statements on the Kashmir controversy. At one point Mawdudi was imprisoned, sentenced to death, reprieved and given a term of fourteen years' imprisonment instead. He was eventually freed after twenty-six months.

When the first constitution was issued in 1956, Mawdudi and the Islamic Organisation accepted it. This constitution was, however, a compromise between the more liberal political leadership and their Western-minded bureaucrats on the one hand and the conservative religious groups on the other. It would not satisfy many for long.

Under martial law from 1958 to 1962 all political activity was prohibited. The 1956 constitution was suspended and President Muhammad Ayub Khan sought to curb the power of the religious leaders. When political opinions were allowed free expression, Mawdudi campaigned for the reinstatement of a constitution which was more Islamic. In 1962, the Islamic provisions of 1956 were substantially restored.

In 1973, Prime Minister Zulfiqar Ali Bhutto's Pakistan People's Party (PPP) advocated a type of Islamic socialism. His programme of secularisation provoked strong opposition from the Islamic Organisation and its supporters in the country. As a concession, the 1973 constitution decreed that Islam should be the state religion, that the president should be a Muslim and that within seven years all laws should be in conformity with Islam. The concession, however, proved merely to be a cosmetic exercise with other issues dominating the political agenda in Pakistan under Bhutto.

General Zia ul-Haq's programme of Islamisation of the state proceeded from his 1977 coup with strong approval from Mawdudi until the latter's death in 1979. Of all the major reformist visionaries with strong influence in the formulating of recent policies in Pakistan, it is Mawdudi who has had most effect. His society remained a strong pressure group on the military regime until Zia's own death. Such pressure resulted in the reintroduction of traditional Islamic punishments for various crimes. It also led to the attempt to form an effective Islamic banking system.

The Islamic Organisation, and Mawdudi in particular, had significant influence on the development of Muslim resurgent movements in other parts of the world. Mawdudi's major works were translated from Urdu and English into Arabic in the 1950s, and he himself met Sayyid Qutb in Cairo in 1951. In the Middle East, the events in Palestine in 1948 caused a lot of Muslim soul-searching and Mawdudi's call for renewed submission to God's rule seemed to point out an area that had been deficient in all the clamouring for independence from colonial powers.

Today the leadership of the Islamic Organisation has passed into non-idealist hands. A major tension exists between the surviving theoreticians, mainly Karachi-based, and the Punjab-based pragmatists. The pragmatists are led by Mian Tufail Muhammad, Amir of the society and successor to Mawdudi. His objective under Zia was to wring concessions from the military regime through political dialogue. The student wing of the Organisation, the *Islâmî-Jamâ'at-i Ṭulâba*, also acts as a paramilitary force, maintaining an armed presence on university campuses.

The weak and the strong

Mawdudi's goal, then, was consistently clear. He argued and lobbied for the establishment of an Islamic state. The setting for that state was the Indian subcontinent after the departure of the British. With partition, Muslims in some areas of the subcontinent would become 'the strong', able to determine their own destinies. In their midst, however, would likely live 'the weak', the minority groups. In an Islamic state such as that which Mawdudi had in mind, how should such minorities be handled?

Mawdudi wrote a treatise on this subject in August 1948, a year after the founding of Pakistan. Its intended readership was the body of experts entrusted with writing a constitution for that new country. Mawdudi's dealing with non-Muslim minorities hangs, of course, upon his conception of an Islamic state. That conception is summarised in Figure 9. The contrast with a national state highlights the significant points of departure in Mawdudi's mind. Such contrast also serves to explain the recurring sense of insecurity among Christians and Hindus in contemporary Pakistan.

Mawdudi had very much in his mind the 'hypocrisy' of the national state model as he saw it being expressed in India, Palestine and Algeria in the late 1940s. He far preferred the openness of the Islamic state model which made quite clear what were the rights of the non-Muslims (*dhimmîs*) living within its confines. Figure 10 summarises those rights.[14]

Mawdudi was a theoretician whose ideas remain foundational in many Islamic reformists' manifestos today. Like many theoreticians who propose their programmes as part of an alternative to the existing status quo, Mawdudi was not put in the position of having to work through his suggestions. He never knew the headaches of trying to institutionalise his ideals. Indeed, wry comments followed his support of Fatima Jinnah's candidacy for the presidency of Pakistan in 1964 in opposition to Ayub Khan. Wasn't Mawdudi supposed to be a proponent of the traditional closeted role for

An Islamic State	A National State
Muslims: believe in the principles on which the state is founded	Majority: connected with the class which founded the state
Non-Muslims: do not believe in those principles	Minorities: not so connected
Muslims only will belong to the government	Only supporters fill roles of governing and maintaining justice
Clear-cut distinction made between Muslims and non-Muslims	In reality a discrimination between majority and minorities
Precise rights guaranteed to non-Muslims, but no participation in responsibility for justice	Absorption of minorities in the majority culture *or* manipulation till minority emigrates *or* subjugation till minority accepts to live without rights
Muslims must confer on non-Muslims all the rights outlined in Islamic law (*sharīʿa*)	No constraint on majority to grant rights to those with minority status; usually rights are restricted by majority

Figure 9
Mawdudi's comparison of an Islamic state with a National state

Muslim women? Theory and political expediency meshed only with difficulty. In his writings, Mawdudi doesn't enter into a detailed discussion of the precise limits of freedom in the Islamic state. Nor does he explain how a state may both control everything and yet leave a large area of conduct to individual discretion.

Statement of Right	Explanation
Protection of the person	The blood of non-Muslims is like that of Muslims. If a Muslim kills a non-Muslim he is punished in the same manner as for killing a Muslim.
Freedom of speech	Non-Muslims enjoy basic freedoms: of speech, of writing, of assembly, of celebration of feasts to the same degree as Muslims. They may also develop their religious allegiances, with freedom to convert from one non-Islamic to another non-Islamic variety (Muslims may not so change). Non-Muslims may act in accordance with their conscience so long as they remain within the law of the state.
Access to education	Same rules apply to non-Muslims as to Muslims concerning compulsory education. Non-Muslims will not have to receive Muslim religious instruction but can arrange their own forms.
Privilege of office	Access to all government offices except those deemed 'principal': ie, those at an important level in the ideological organisation of Islam. Similarly, in the armed forces, combat posts are reserved to Muslims.

Figure 10
The rights of non-Muslims (Dhimmîs) according to Mawdudi

Mawdudi's vision of an Islamic state leans strongly on the supposition that its leaders will be undoubted men of pure Islamic calibre; perhaps such a hope is a little far-fetched in our fallen world. Perhaps it also fails to read Islamic history accurately, for the tendency to move away from the 'ideal' Medinan model of statehood, after the Prophet's death, very much revolved around the quality of those early leaders of the faithful. Lesser mortals soon accommodated themselves to situations which were less than 'ideal'.

Mawdudi hoped, through the Islamic Organisation, to produce a kind of faithful Islamic yeast in the new society of Pakistan which would irreversibly leaven the whole land.

CHAPTER SEVEN

A BLOODY AFFAIR!

'**D**AMN THE BRITISH! Damn the Hindus! Damn the Sikhs! Damn India!'

Old Kasim muttered at the dully painted walls of his bedroom. Saliva trickled down his chin as the verbal explosions died on the tip of his tongue. His weak condition forced the anger to surface as a hiss of despair disguising the man's acute hatred for those responsible, in his view, for the bloody mess so many years ago.

Kasim's children had long since slipped from the bedside of the dying man. Their mother had beckoned them away as she sensed her husband losing control.

'Don't let him die like this!' she prayed as she squeezed the children down the hall to the living room. 'Don't let the children remember him so distraught.'

With a glance back towards the bedroom, Ruxsana busied herself with producing food for the youngsters' hungry mouths. As she worked, calling instructions to her daughter, Ruxsana thought back over the last few months.

Her husband's illness had progressively worsened and as it did so it seemed to heave up from the depths of his memory vivid recollections. It was as if his body could no longer be taught to ignore the ulceration of his spirit. Coarse acids burned their way through stomach and intestines. Dark bile rose from the pit of the man, mimicking the spasms of anger and disgust hissed through parched lips. How could she, Ruxsana, ever understand what Kasim had experienced, those many years past? She had always lived in Lahore. She had seen nothing of what he saw.

Partition!

With increasing frequency in the waning months of his life, Kasim returned to those memories of 1947. Or rather, those memories kept returning to him, for he would never willingly have called them up. Mountbatten's boundary commission had ruled that a Muslim majority area could only be part of Pakistan if it lay next to other areas also to be included in Pakistan. Many people found themselves on the wrong side of the new border. In Punjab, where Kasim lived, the presence of the holy city of Amritsar ensured that the Sikhs would also be involved in the upheavals of massive population exchange.

The relief of final escape and eventual security in the new nation were eclipsed in Kasim's mind by the mental replays of those days of train-waiting, eventual boarding and noisy steaming off towards....

An hour into the uncomfortable, crowded journey and Kasim's carriage is jolted, shaken, slowed down. Buffers jab and relax, jab and relax as the steel worm, crawling with families inside, outside and on top, is brought to a halt in the middle of nowhere. Steel and concrete cross the tracks up ahead. An uncanny silence is broken only by the steamy hiss of pausing engine.

The questionings in the carriages grow, shouting to those on top, asking what the cause of delay is now. Murmured, incoherent replies float down. Temperature and tempers rise in the packed compartments.

Suddenly, a wave of horror ripples over the curved roofs of the dormant train. 'A massacre! O my God, it's a massacre! Get away from the train! Get away!'

Shouts and screams deafen the desert. People jump down,

others clamber up in futile contradiction. Neither roof nor ground offers sanctuary for long. Women and children fall out of carriage doorways, trampling one another in a hopeless stampede away from what had been, till a moment ago, their passport to a new life. Now that motionless passport, passive, is being savagely turned into a shattered, mangled, mass coffin.

Strange men clamber aboard, surge down the train, compartment by compartment—a systematic death machine—scything here, stabbing there, laughing and sweating as blood spurts in their faces, down their clothes, over their sandals. Others fan outwards from the train sides, a more leisurely procedure, pursuing and abusing the female and baby desert-seekers: no refuge here, you poor creatures, just a double dying. Life and honour choke to death in the scrub.

Kasim jerks his head away! An arm lies alone on the dirt beside him, blood still oozing. Its mother-torso covers him, presses on him, dead weight crushing his chest but miraculously proffering him life. Both belong to Saleem, his oldest cousin. A cousin in pieces! Oh no, Saleem! Mourning begins early in Kasim's charmed life.

Eventually the groans diminish around him. The killing time is over, the dying minutes nearly gone. Kasim shifts his cousin's corpse from on top of him and cautiously lifts his head. He sees and yet cannot afford to see the afterbirth scattered around him. Faces with eyes gouged out, stripped women, split babies, vomit everywhere and blood, gallons of it, poured in unstinting libation to the gods of partition.

From this torn desert womb Kasim emerges, limping, running, salt-eyed, thirsty, lost. Somehow he reaches Lahore. Somehow he alone of his family makes it to the new nation. Somehow he works and marries and learns to forget....

Years back, Kasim the orphan-refugee started a new life. He was one more Pakistani, baptised in blood. Now he knows those days revisited. He twists and curses in the dying upheavals of his whole being, body and soul.

'Oh for the peace that would wipe the unthinkable from my mind, some balm that would caress away the locked-in memories. Ruxsana, bless her, serves me well enough, but no human hands can remould the cancered core of a survivor of partition. I doubt even God can.'

Ruxsana, bless her, busy with chapatti preparation in the kitchen, hoped and prayed for her dying husband Kasim that God could do just that.

CHAPTER EIGHT

THE LAND OF THE PURE

Farewell to the *Râj*!

IN THE MOVES TOWARDS INDEPENDENCE in India after World War II, both Hindus and Muslims wanted the British out. For a considerable time a united 'Indian' India was visualised. Gradually, however, it became clear that the two communities would not accommodate one another: unless there was partition there would be civil war. In 1946, both Congress and the Muslim League rejected the British suggestions for a federated government. Partition was their choice and the months left to the British were spent in sorting out boundaries. 'Divide and quit' became the name of the British game from March to August 1947.[15] On 14 August, Pakistan became a nation, followed a day later by the independent state of India.

Pakistan—'the land of the pure'—was established on the philosophy that the Muslims of India comprised a distinct nation and therefore needed a territorial homeland. The major proponent of this idea was the Muslim League under its opportunist director Muhammad Ali Jinnah. It was Jinnah who, as 'Great Founder' (*Qâ'id-i 'Azam*), set the tone for the emerging state. Not all Muslim Pakistanis, however, agreed with Jinnah's perspective.

Whose Pakistan?

The people of the new Pakistan were sharply divided by ethnic, linguistic, ideological and religious differences. In the western part of the nation, more than half the people were Punjabis, but some 20 per cent were Sindhis, 13 per cent Pathans and 3-4 per cent Baluchis. Bengal in the east was like a nation within a nation.

The appeal to a shared Muslim heritage was sufficient to unite the Muslims against the British and to move the majority of them to demand a homeland independent of the Hindus. It was not enough to suppress the variety of regional nationalisms, class differences and varying Islamic allegiances within the new nation. A brief summary of the major events in the years following the establishment of Pakistan exposes the width of that variety. Figure 11 highlights some of the birthpangs of this complex new nation.

From the outset, no clear national identity emerged. Indeed, within three decades the new nation had broken violently in half.

Whose 'Islam'?

The 'pure' in Pakistan were the Muslims. The country was deliberately consolidated as an Islamic state in order to make it different from the remainder of the subcontinent. The people's Muslim identity, however, did not prove cohesive enough to unite the nation internally. Too many of the 'pure' had different ideas as to what their Muslim identity entailed.

Jinnah, for example, deliberately minimised the Islamic component in his vision for the new, independent state of Pakistan. He really had in mind a secular state. Theocratic ideas were anathema to him. In his inaugural address to the Pakistan Constituent Assembly in August 1947, three days before Pakistan came into being, he declared:

You may belong to any religion or caste or creed—that has nothing to do with the business of the state...we are all citizens of one state.... In the course of time Hindus will cease to be Hindus and Muslims will cease to be Muslims, not in the religious sense because that is the personal faith of each individual but in the political sense, as citizens of the state.[16]

The secular principle was Jinnah's foundation stone in the building of Pakistan.

In the view of reformists like Mawdudi, a very different principle prevailed. Under the British *Râj*, India had ceased to be the domain of Muslim faith and practice (*dâr al-Islâm*). Although Muslims had been allowed to practise the tenets of their faith, political power had been removed from them. Queen Victoria was their ruler, not a Muslim sovereign, and certainly not (through the Muslim leader) God himself. Islam had been reduced to merely a form of piety. It was no longer an expression of a way of life.

With the founding of Pakistan, Mawdudi hoped that the new nation would become part of the 'house of Islam' (*dâr al-Islâm*), an Islamic state with primary orientation towards the reformist ideology of Islam. Towards that end he and his élitist society worked.

Mawdudi also felt that the success of Jinnah's view compromised the quality of life for the 50 million or so Muslims left as a minority in India. For them, there would be no chance of living under a truly Islamic form of government. Indeed, as the conflicts between Pakistan and India unfolded in the years following independence, the Muslim minority in India was considered a potential fifth column by the government there.

For the majority of illiterate Muslims in Pakistan, Islam remained the way of life it had always been: a mixture of surface allegiance to orthodox Islam and an underlying commitment to holy men and shrine visitation.

Date	Significant Events
1947	Pakistan independent on 14 August, one day before India. Created from northwestern and northeastern parts of India where Muslims comprise the majority of the population. 6 million Hindus and Sikhs flee from Pakistan to India while 7 million Muslims leave India to travel to Pakistan. Muhammad Ali Jinnah, the Great Founder (*Qâ'id-i 'Azam*), is the first head of government.
1948	India and Pakistan at war over Kashmir until ceasefire in following year.
1951	Census reveals 33.7 million West Pakistanis and 41.9 million East Pakistanis.
1953	Anti-Ahmadîya riots.
1956	Pakistan becomes a Republic with Major General Iskender Mirza elected first President.
1958	General Ayub Khan takes over to root out corruption and end chaotic civilian rule.
1965	Renewed fighting over Kashmir: Pakistan defeated. Provincial autonomy demanded for Bengal.
1969	General Yahya Khan takes charge, imposing martial law.
1970	Cyclone and tidal wave strikes East Pakistan and over 200,000 are killed. Many East Pakistanis accuse the government of delaying shipments of food and relief supplies. The whole of Pakistan elects a National Assembly with a brief to draft a new constitution. East Pakistan has 56% of the population and therefore a majority of Assembly members. Those East Pakistan members elected belong to the secular Awami League wanting some self-government for their section of Pakistan. In West Pakistan the Pakistan People's Party gets a landslide victory in Sind and Punjab and the left-wing National Awami Party does well in Sarhad and Baluchistan. The Islamic parties make a poor showing.

Date	Significant Events
1971	In March, President Yahya Khan postpones the first meeting of the National Assembly. The East Pakistanis demonstrate noisily and the army is ordered into East Pakistan. Civil war follows and later in March, East Pakistan declares itself an independent nation: Bangladesh. In December, India joins Bangladesh against West Pakistan until eventually Pakistan surrenders. More than 1 million people die.
	Yahya Khan resigns and Zulfiqar Ali Bhutto, the head of the Pakistan People's Party (PPP), succeeds him. The PPP espouses an Islamic socialism.
	Opposition to Bhutto takes on a strongly Islamic tone under the slogan *Niẓâm-i Mustafa* ('Give us the political system of Prophet Muhammad!').
1973	New constitution is published and Bhutto becomes Pakistan's Prime Minister in an Islamic Republic.
1977	Elections result in victory for Bhutto's political party but there are strong allegations of election fraud.
	In July, military leaders remove Bhutto from office. General Zia ul-Haq takes over control of the government. Exploits Islamic ideology to legitimate state power in the hands of the military. Islamisation of the state proceeds with state-sponsored schemes for the *ḥajj*, the collection of *zakât* and the enforcement of fasting during Ramaḍân.
1978	Military government convicts Bhutto of ordering the murder of a political opponent while he was serving as Prime Minister. Sentenced to death and executed the following year.
1980	Pakistan's laws (except those to do with the working of the economy) Islamised by the Constitution (Amendment) Order 1980, setting up *sharî'a* courts.

Figure 11
Birthpangs of a nation

Tug-of-war

The struggle between competing views of the role of Islam in the new Pakistan has dogged politics there from the 1940s to the 1990s. Meanwhile a Punjabi élite of soldiers, administrators and landowners has, for the most part, retained its hold on the strings of power.

During the ascendancy of secularists like Jinnah and Bhutto, Mawdudi's Islamic Organisation (*Jamâʿat-i Islâmî*) took the role of agitator. It opposed the landlords, businessmen, officials and Sufi leaders who stood to benefit from the separation of politics and religion.

The period of Zia ul-Haq's rule saw a radical increase in Mawdudi's influence. Not long after seizing power, General Zia declared that he had experienced 'inspiration' (*ilhâm*), a special state in which he had received a message from God. He reported that he was being charged with the task of creating an Islamic state in Pakistan. This was precisely the brief long promoted by Mawdudi. His Islamic Organisation acquired a strong voice in the universities and the educational system, and in the government-controlled broadcasting media. Considerable steps towards the realisation of Mawdudi's vision for Pakistan were taken during General Zia's period in office.

Not all was straightforward, however. By 1982, the new leader of the Islamic Organisation was complaining that the recommendations of the Council of Islamic Ideology were not being implemented. One retired Supreme Court judge named B.Z. Kaikaus had filed a petition before the *Sharîʿa* Bench of the Lahore High Court complaining that the government of General Zia had done little to Islamise Pakistan's political system. The case was dismissed amid national publicity.

The Islamic Organisation had been considerably hampered by its shallow roots in Pakistani society. Being essentially an élitist group of educated individuals, its concerns for reconstructing society have often failed to capture the imagination of ordinary Muslims in Pakistan. The controlled elections orchestrated by the Zia regime in January 1985 dramatically demonstrated that credibility gap. At the elections, all opposition parties were under a ban and their leaders in exile or jail. Yet the Organisation was marginalised in the political arena.

The election of a woman (with a Sindhi power base) to a brief premiership after Zia suggests that the issue of Punjabi national dominance is as critical an issue as Islamisation in contemporary Pakistani politics. The army, controlled by Punjabi officers, may seek validation in the ideology of Mawdudi's Organisation, but the electorate, especially in Sindh province, has other concerns in mind. Such regional protest against Punjabi domination will continue to find expression however strongly the Punjabis identify their rule with that of an Islamic state.

Those ladies!

Muslim family law, dealing with marriage, divorce and inheritance, brings the *sharî'a* (sacred law) home to every household. In many ways, family law comprises the kernel of the *sharî'a*, touching all Muslims. In Pakistan, family law had been reformed in the years since partition. Such reform had taken place, not by replacing Islamic rules with Western-based codes, but by reinterpreting parts of Islamic legal tradition. Child marriage and polygamy had been restricted while grounds for divorce had been revised and rationalised.

The role of women has become a touchstone of religious and political tensions in Pakistan. Mawdudi's Organisation especially has made the issue of 'women' the major yardstick by which it has measured the process of Islamisation in the country. The 1980s saw the emergence of men such as Dr Israr Ahmed, with his media-conveyed attacks on the 'liberal' and 'unIslamic' status of women in Pakistan.[17] That decade also saw a growth in women's movements in the country, movements which organised marches and demonstrations and political rallies. Eventually Benazir Bhutto, the daughter of the late Zulfiqar Ali Bhutto, was elected and survived for nearly two years as a female Prime Minister in an Islamic state. Her demise, moreover, was not particularly due to her being a female. Miss Bhutto inherited a weak economy and the largest refugee problem in the world. She did not have an overall majority in the National Assembly and was unable to repeal Zia's amendment to the constitution which gave more power to the President than to the Prime Minister.

Fatally flawed?

Since its creation, Pakistan has known a variety of constitutions, and a series of civilian and military rules. Islam certainly provided an initial sense of identity in pre-partition India *vis-à-vis* the British or the Hindus. In the resulting Islamic country, however, a diversity of concepts as to what is meant by an Islamic state has emerged.

Despite his influential contribution to the worldwide movement of Islamic resurgence, Mawdudi's vision for Pakistan remains only one aspiration among several. The land of the pure is too compromised by ethnic, linguistic and ideological distinctions to allow the dominance of one all-embracing approach to religio-political expression.

For the foreseeable future it would seem that Pakistan will remain the home of the less than pure.

CHAPTER NINE

BY THE WATERS OF ISMAILIYA

Martyr for a cause

THE SETTING IS A STREET IN CAIRO in the late afternoon of 12 February 1949. A forty-three-year-old Egyptian steps out onto the pavement. He has just finished consulting with friends after being mysteriously summoned to the headquarters of the Young Men's Muslim Association. As he climbs into a taxi, shots explode from close at hand. The man is checked in mid-step, then collapses into the car. He dies a few minutes later in a nearby hospital.

Already acknowledged by his followers as an *imâm* or religious leader, Ḥasan al-Bannâ's assassination transformed him into a *shahîd* or martyr. His assassins, it eventually turned out, were members of the secret police. Five years later, under a different government, they were brought to trial and heavily sentenced.

Ḥasan al-Bannâ' (Banna) was the founder and first 'guide' (*murshid*) of the Muslim Brotherhood, *Al-Ikhwân al-Muslimûn*.

Watch-repairer's son

Hasan al-Banna was born in October 1906 in the small delta town of Mahmûdîya to a pious family. His father was a graduate of Al-Azhar University and an author of books on Islamic law and traditions. He was known locally as 'the watch-mender' (*al-Sâʿâtî*). The old man passed on both his practical skills and his Islamic learning and piety to his son.

Banna grew up in difficult times for Egyptians. After the end of World War I, Egyptians revolted strongly against the British protectorate and won semi-independent status in 1922. A couple of years later, however, the whole of the Muslim world was shaken by the abolition of the caliphate. Atatürk's deliberate secularisation of Turkey allowed no room for the previous political centre of Islamic authority in Istanbul. Islam as a world force seemed to have lost its way. Equivalent leanings towards secularisation were strong in academic circles in Egypt. Christian missionary work seemed to be encroaching on traditional Islamic ways of educating young Egyptians.

Teacher of Arabic

Banna was given a traditional early education and then moved to Cairo to pursue a career in teaching. He graduated in 1927 from the main institute in Egypt for training teachers of Arabic. Banna's four years in Cairo as a student confirmed his sense of vocation: he felt that Egyptian young people were inheriting a very corrupted form of Islam.

Banna began his teaching career in Ismailiya, a town alongside the Suez Canal. He remained in the profession until his resignation in 1946, nineteen years later. In Ismailiya, the young teacher experienced firsthand the vast economic difference between the European town and the indigenous quarter. He grew to hate the military power of the British and was sickened by the dominating economic role of the Suez Canal Company.

One day, six discontented Egyptian labourers from the British camp expressed to Banna their similar disillusionment. What was wrong with Islam that their lot had sunk so low? Where had Muslims gone wrong?

Reformer of society

Banna could sit silent no longer. Together the seven men took an oath to be troops (*jund*) for the message of Islam. Banna christened the group 'the Muslim Brothers'. So the Muslim Brotherhood began in embryo form in the 'native' quarter of Ismailiya at the end of the 1920s.

For three years the group sought to enlarge its membership in and around Ismailiya. This was achieved by sponsoring discussions in public places and focusing on moral and social reform, especially among youth.

In 1932, Banna obtained a transfer to Cairo. When he moved to the capital, the headquarters of the Brotherhood moved with him. Over the next eight years the Society grew into one of the most important political contestants on the Egyptian scene. By 1940 it had 500 branches, each with its own centre, a mosque, a school and a club or home industry. Its membership included significant numbers of civil servants, students, urban labourers and peasants.

Asking too much?

In the post-war years, Hasan al-Banna urged the Egyptian authorities to declare a holy war against the rule of the British in Egypt. In 1948 he sent cadres of Brothers to fight against Zionist forces in Palestine. His Society was eventually dissolved by decree later that year, the government fearing its role in the widespread destabilising of Egyptian society. Nuqrashi Pasha, the Prime Minister responsible for the banning, was assassinated within months in the Ministry of Interior by a Muslim Brother. Banna predicted that the government would retaliate. In less than eight weeks he himself was dying from bullet wounds on a taxi floor.

The revolutionary from a little delta town went to his grave escorted by tanks and armoured cars, though with only his immediate family allowed to attend the funeral.

Rotten to the core

Hasan al-Banna had very specific goals for the Muslim Brotherhood. Those goals arose out of his view of what was wrong with the world of Islam.

The rottenness which Banna smelled all around him was depicted most sharply in the shortcomings of the Al-Azhar theologians and scholars. Banna felt that this leading voice of Muslims worldwide had failed to remain the spokesman for a pure and dynamic Islam. Instead, the personnel of Al-Azhar had themselves imbibed foreign ideas and values and led the way in a retreat from Islam as it was intended. As a consequence, Egypt had fallen into religious, cultural, political, economic, social and moral decadence.

Banna perceived that Egypt was at a crossroads. Which way would the country choose to go: the way of the West or the way of Islam? Banna wrote to King Farûq about the urgency of the situation . . .

Internationalism, nationalism, socialism, capitalism, Bolshevism, war, the distribution of wealth, the link between producer and consumer, and whatever is intimately or distantly tied up with the discussions which preoccupy the statesmen of the nations and the social philosophers—we believe that all of these have been dealt with thoroughly by Islam. . . .[18]

Islam was all-embracing, the answer to Egypt's problems and the world's problems. Hasan al-Banna offered his movement as a vanguard to help bring back the true Islam.

True Islam the only answer

The pure Islam towards which Banna urged Farûq was the Islam of the Muslim Brotherhood. Their Islam was not limited to worship and ritual or mere 'spirituality'. It was a robust Islam, touching all the affairs of people in this world and in the hereafter. Their Islam included the virtues of all other systems and was sufficient in itself for the rebirth of Egypt.

Twentieth-century Muslims needed to return to the Islamic principles of the first Muslims. What had inspired those original believers so much? The Qur'ân! The Qur'ân was the inclusive book which gathered together the fundamentals of faith, the foundations for proper social life and the only appropriate basis for human law. The Qur'ân is constantly quoted in Banna's lectures and tracts.

The stated goal in view was the creation of an Islamic order (*al-nizâm al-islâmî*). In practice, this slogan meant roughly 'a Muslim state'. It is significant that, by and large, Banna, his successor Hudaybi and many of the early Brothers felt that the existing constitutional parliamentary framework in Egypt could, with some reformation, satisfy the political requirements of Islam for a 'Muslim state'. The main nub of their demands was for the replacement of Western codes by Islamic law (*sharî'a*). The state needed to return to revelation as the source of its life and to abandon the current separation of 'religion' and politics.

Banna and the Society sought to 'guide' the government by advocating a series of reform programmes. They also sought to demonstrate the validity of their perspectives by modelling social reorganisation based on Islamic principles.

Banna's approach was therefore that of a gradualist. He was a gifted orator and sought to persuade his immediate and distant audiences of the rightness and feasibility of his calls for reform. As the movement and momentum developed, some members favoured a more activist approach. In 1939, for example, one group (known as

'Muḥammad's Boys' or *Shabâb Muḥammad*) split from Banna, impatient for action against the authorities.

What about *jihâd*?

The Muslim Brotherhood as led by Hasan al-Banna and his immediate successor, al-Hudaybi, was primarily a political movement. In both 1948 and 1954 the Society was legally dissolved and strongly repressed by the governments of the day. The main official reason given on each occasion was that the Brotherhood was plotting to assume political power. In both cases, however, the mass of documents throws doubt on the claim that the Society's leadership was planning such extreme action. Under the directorship of Banna, certainly, the message was constantly given that, at least officially, the aim of the Brotherhood was not to come to power, but to assist in the reform of society.

The bringing back of true Islam or the reforming of society obviously necessitated a struggle, even if that struggle was only 'political'. Were there some conditions in which a more outright militancy could be included? Banna dealt with the matter of *jihâd* (holy war) in a tract, the emphases of which are summarised in Figure 12.[19] In the period 1945 to 1952, many groups in Egypt resorted to violence. The Nuqrashi government of the time was very repressive and invited strong reaction. The Muslim Brotherhood participated with many Egyptians in such reaction. The Brothers' motivation was unique in respect of their 'Islamic' focus. Their intolerance of revolutionaries with other motivations also set the Brotherhood apart.

Above all, *jihâd* is a divine command. Banna insisted that, in contrast to the murderous kind of warfare engaged in by the so-called 'civilised' world powers of the twentieth century, *jihâd* is to be conducted in a merciful way. *Jihâd* may well involve martyrdom. Banna makes the point that we all

Jihâd	Exposition
An inescapable duty	As firmly established as any other of the 'pillars' of the faith
Authentication	From: Qur'ânic texts the Traditions (*hadîth*) the four schools of law
The aim	To guide mankind to the truth until God's Word is seen to be done
Methodology	The end does not justify all means and mercy is necessary in pursuit of the goal

Figure 12
Al-Bannâ' on jihâd *(holy war)*

have to die. So why not die in the most glorious way possible, committed to *jihâd*? 'If you suffer it in the way of God, it will be to your profit in this world, and your reward in the next.'[20]

In Banna's preaching, *jihâd* does have a strong physical connotation. It is not just a *jihâd* of the spirit. It has to be conducted, it would seem, by militant means, by the use of arms. However, it has to be tempered by an approach which is merciful. Even in *jihâd*, Banna's aim is for the Brotherhood to be educative, an example of how true Muslims behave. The successors to Banna would move a long way from the Brotherhood's founder in regard to their understanding of *jihâd*.

The preacher

Hasan al-Banna was influenced in his thinking by Jamâl al-Dîn al-Afghânî and Muhammad 'Abduh.[21] He wanted to see a restoration of the Islamic world-state. He wanted to see an

Islamic march to conquer the rest of the earth for God's Word. He especially wanted to see the poison of the Western worldview with its 'freedoms' and lax sexual standards abolished from Muslim communities. The People of the Book (Christians and Jews) would only live peaceably in Banna's new society as they accepted a second-class status. The 'corrupt' Muslim rulers would not be allowed to live at all. They were as much enemies of God's Word to al-Banna as the Europeans. To them al-Banna shouted, along with Rashîd Riḍâ whom he admired so much: 'Back to the Qur'ân and the *sunna*!'

Banna stunned his listeners with his straightforward eloquence. Ḥasan Ismâ´îl al-Ḥudaybi, a judge who became successor to Banna in leading the Muslim Brotherhood, first listened to the preacher in 1944:

> How many speeches have I heard, hoping each time that they could speedily end.... This time, I feared that Hasan al-Banna would end his speech.... One hundred minutes passed, and he collected the hearts of the Muslims in the palms of his hands...and shook them as he willed.... The speech ended, and he returned to his listeners their hearts...except for mine, which remained in his hand.[22]

It was not just would-be recruits who listened carefully to Hasan al-Banna. One young officer, at that time urging on a revolution to topple the monarchy in Egypt, responded enthusiastically to his first meeting with the Supreme Guide of the Muslim Brotherhood. The encounter took place in an army communications barracks in a southern suburb of Cairo during the feast of the prophet's birthday (*Mawlid al-Nabî*). The twenty-four-year lieutenant was entranced by the strange figure with sad and dreamy eyes and bizarre clothes. He was more than entranced by the man's conversation:

> He talked chiefly on religious topics, but not in the accustomed manner of the preacher, with sonorous phrases and learned

references. He went straight to the nub of the question, and he spoke with directness and ease. It seemed strange to me, but here was a theologian with a sense of reality, a man of religion who recognised the existence of facts.[23]

Anwar al-Sâdât, the officer concerned, would one day find himself the target of *jihâd*. His assassins would be young Egyptians influenced by the 'new radical' successors to Hasan al-Banna.

CHAPTER TEN

THE GODFATHER

Impossible to silence

A N UNMARKED GRAVE IN A SECRET BURIAL PLOT hides the last remains of another Egyptian. He was a small, dark, softly spoken man, sensitive and very intense. His recorded words have inspired numerous revivalist movements throughout the Muslim world. Within his native land his writings have had a strong impact on Islamic groups, especially after 1971 when President Sadat allowed those groups to resume their activities. His name was Sayyid Qutb.

Like Banna, Sayyid Qutb was born in 1906. His birthplace was the village of Qaha, in Asyut province. His father was a gentleman farmer who had been on pilgrimage at Mecca. By the age of ten, Sayyid Qutb had memorised the entire Qur'ân. Three years later he was sent to an uncle in Cairo to continue his education. Sayyid Qutb developed a strong interest in English literature and himself wrote a lot of poetry and stories. After graduation he was appointed an inspector in the Ministry of Education, a position he eventually gave up in order to devote himself to writing.

A poet's 'U'-turn

For a man so strongly attracted to Western literature, the 1940s proved a painful time of reassessment and eventual conversion. British war policies during World War II did not seem to favour the aspiration of Egyptians, while the creation of the State of Israel in the aftermath of the war thoroughly disillusioned Qutb. He felt that the Western world was denying to the Arabs the right of self-determination. Such feelings were reinforced during Qutb's visit to the USA in 1949 where he witnessed the massive American media support for Israel. He also experienced some personal discrimination.

When he returned to Egypt, Qutb joined the Muslim Brotherhood and began writing on Islamic topics. A lot of his compositions in this period were to provide the foundation for an Islamic ideology. That ideology was deliberately designed to make redundant those of communism, capitalism, nationalism, liberalism and secularism. Qutb was quite strongly influenced by the thought of Mawdudi, whose writings became available in Egypt in 1951.

In 1952 there was an army coup against King Farûq. The Free Officers responsible involved the Muslim Brotherhood in the coup itself. Afterwards, when the officers banned all political parties, they exempted the Muslim Brotherhood on the grounds that it was a religious body. Indeed, the officers sent for Sayyid Qutb who functioned as a consultant to them for six months.

Praise to prison

In 1953 Nasser eased Neguib out of the supreme leadership role and began to implement land reform throughout the country. The Brotherhood was opposed to such change and soon Sayyid Qutb withdrew his support for the officers. He realised that the new government did not really want to establish an Islamic state.

Qutb wrote several books at this time dealing with his understanding of the Islamic view of reality. In 1954 a militant Brother, motivated by Qutb's ideological stance, tried to assassinate Nasser at a rally in Alexandria. He failed and was executed along with five others. Many were jailed, including Sayyid Qutb; his sentence was fifteen years of hard labour.

While he was in prison, Qutb completed a vast commentary on the Qur'ân and wrote several other books. He also developed a strong friendship with Yusuf Hawwash who would become Qutb's deputy in the resurrected clandestine Muslim Brotherhood. After ten years of prison, Qutb was released by Nasser as the result of the intercession of the then President of Iraq. A few months after his release, Qutb's most controversial book, *Signposts on the Road (Maʿâlim Fîʾl-Ṭarîq)*, was published in November 1964.

In *Signposts*, Qutb set out some of his radical conclusions. Society he divided into two kinds: the order of Islam and the order of *jâhilîya*. The latter order was 'ignorant' and debased, like the type which had existed in Arabia before Prophet Muhammad's revolution there. Such an order was visible in the world today in the Western nations. Qutb declared that Western societies are images of the future for Muslims. Muslim societies would become like the West as the world grows smaller. Muslims need to inoculate themselves against such 'cultural poisoning' by re-establishing the kingdom of God on earth. Qutb accused Nasser's regime of fast slipping into *jâhilîya* disorder. Moral reformation was the urgent need of the hour and it was to be achieved by a *jihâd* (holy war) against Westernisation.

Qutb was quickly rearrested, his writings associated with three alleged plots to kill Nasser. The police crackdown netted fewer than 250 activists. It was the new message borne by the group, rather than the number of people involved, that worried the authorities. The prosecution produced a major analysis of *Signposts* as the basis for accusation in court.

At his trial, Qutb did not deny the charge of sedition. He claimed that he had a higher allegiance than to patriotism based on geographical region. 'Homeland' for him was not a piece of God's earth but the community of believers, God's party. The current problems of Egypt lay wholly with the government which had opted for a way contrary to the way of God.

Qutb spoke out in the period after direct colonial rule. His concern was the internal faithlessness of the house of Islam. He challenged the newly established revolutionary Republic saying that its anti-imperialistic credentials, its close contacts with the Muslim Brotherhood and its lower middle-class origin were not enough. The secularising tendency in Nasserism represented the throwing off of God's sovereignty in all areas of life. Such rot must be stopped at all costs. Qutb was condemned to death in 1966 and executed.

There was a sting in the tail of the story however. Within a year of Qutb's execution a six-day war had occurred in the Middle East. That short, sharp war saw the humiliation of vast Arab forces at the hands of little Israel. The semisecular Arab socialism of Nasser was seen to be found wanting and Qutb's thesis prevailed widely among ordinary Egyptians: the Arabs had been defeated because they had turned away from the will of God.

The will of God

Qutb called for the establishment of God's will on earth and its proper maintenance through the application of Islamic law (*shari'a*). Why had God's will been disestablished? Who had diverted major Muslim populations from the way of God? Among the many candidates for blame, including Muslim Presidents and communists, Qutb cites Christians (colonists) and Jews (Zionists). Typical is the following statement from his commentary on the Qur'ân:

> This is the reality of the battle which the Jews and the Christians initiate in every land and at all times against the Islamic community.... It is the battle of doctrine that is raging between the Islamic camp and these two armies who may fight among themselves...however, they always cooperate in the battle against Islam and the Muslims.... They did not announce it a war in the name of doctrine—as it is in reality—fearing the zeal and emotion of the doctrine. Rather, they announced it in the name of land, of economics, of politics, of military bases....[24]

International Zionism, international communism and international crusaderism were all signs of this essential conflict disguised as other issues. Qutb called on his fellow Muslims to stop patterning their lives on the West; the source of that Western model came via the People of the Book. Muslims may only pattern themselves after the mind of God as revealed in the Qur'ân.

From words to war

Qutb's Islamic 'liberation theology' quickly ran out of patience with compromised political authorities, such as those of Nasser's regime. Nasser had put Qutb in prison far too often and much too long. Not only did incarceration and torture breed a desire for revenge; it also forced Qutb and the Brothers to face up to the realities of the new nationalist, military-controlled state. Qutb saw that proclamation would not be enough. Militancy had to provide the answer. A much more violent interpretation of *jihâd* than Banna's became the watchword:

> Truth and falsehood cannot coexist on earth. When Islam makes a general declaration to establish the lordship of God on earth and to liberate humanity from the worship of other creatures, it

is contested by those who have usurped God's sovereignty on earth. They will never make peace. Then [Islam] goes forth destroying them to free humans from their power...this is the constant situation. The liberating struggle of jihad does not cease until all religion belongs to God.... The greatest bondage—in the view of Islam—is subservience to human laws legislated by humans.[25]

Compromise with oppressive powers is not acceptable. Muslims must rise up and take the high ground again. The aim is not 'Egypt' or 'the Arab world'; the goal is the whole world. According to the Qur'ân, God is 'Lord of the worlds'. *Jihâd* is the means for shifting human beings from bondage to anyone or anything to submission to that Lord.

A house fighting against itself?

Qutb has much to say about the question of reformed Muslims attacking other Muslims, especially those in political authority in his own day. The justification for such in-fighting is drawn from Qutb's interpretation of the views of a much respected fourteenth-century Sunnî theologian, Ibn Taimîya.

What does one do as a faithful Muslim if the (Muslim) society in which one lives is in effect a *jâhilî* society? How can an Islamic society be realised where a government brutally suppresses movements like the Muslim Brotherhood and imprisons its leaders?

Qutb's answer is to form a 'state within a state', a mini society, a *jama'a*. Committed believers should band together and dedicate themselves to the bringing in of the true Islamic society. To achieve that level of commitment they need to withdraw from the *jâhilî* society. Such withdrawal Qutb labels 'exodus' (*hijra*) in imitation of Prophet Muhammad's withdrawal from Mecca to Medina. In the small, separated cell of committed believers, true Muslims can prepare to eradicate the apostate prevailing culture and bring in the rule of God. The true Muslims are to be the vanguard of the coming dream. Qutb declared at his trial:

> We are the umma of the Believers, living within a jahili society. Nothing relates us to state or to society and we owe no allegiance to either. As a community of believers we should see ourselves in a state of war with the state and the society. The territory we dwell in is Dar al-Harb [House of War].[26]

Within jails in the late 1960s, Qutb's disciples segregated themselves from other Muslims. They would pray on their own and would refuse to have anything to do with the official *imâms*, or prayer leaders.

As we shall see in Chapter Twelve, the Muslim Brotherhood became eclipsed in the 1970s and 1980s by more radical groups within Egypt. The changing circumstances in the Arab world in the 1950s and 1960s led to a shift in the reformists' approach. Their diagnosis of society's ills now concentrated on the sickness within, especially that of a powerful élite which was guilty of apostasy.

The ideologies of the various Islamic revolutionary groups more recently active within the country take their inspiration largely from Qutb's writings. Gone is the emphasis on long-term education. To the forefront is immediate action. Sayyid Qutb is in many senses 'godfather' to the new radicals.

CHAPTER ELEVEN

KHADIJA'S FREEDOM

A GLOVED HAND STROKED THE BARS of the little window in the heavy cell door. Rough metal caught tiny threads of smooth black silk as Khadija traced the ridges of chipped paint and rust through the delicate, protecting handwear.

'Isn't it funny,' she mused, 'how some see us as doubly imprisoned? Just like my gloved hand—imprisoned within a prison.'

She stretched her hand free of the spiked bars as if to demonstrate that the close-fitting silk was different from the oppressive brick curtains that confined her and her sisters. The glove's soft, sewn walls were protective, the dark prison walls menacing.

'Imprisoned within a prison'—those were very nearly the words used by her college friend Laila on the last occasion they were together before Khadija's arrest.

'You are like a prison within a prison, Khadija! You and your "sisters"! Your bodies are bridled beneath veil and gloves. And your minds are manacled further from sight! Everything is fixed for you, nothing is an exciting experiment any more. It is always "That is forbidden, Laila" or "This is obligatory, Laila." You are fettered, Khadija. Your beautiful body is hidden, and your vitality is all bottled up. You've become a prison within a prison!'

Khadija slapped the scratched metal of the door and laughed out loud, a long joyful trill.

'How wrong you are, dear Laila,' she sang. 'We are free, truly free, freer than ever we were choosing our own way. We follow the *sunna* of Prophet Muhammad, praise be upon him. And that, my love, is perfect freedom!'

The horrors of arrest, the manhandling by secret policemen, even the humiliating words of judges had not managed to diminish Khadija's personal joy. Several months in prison had served only to underline within her soul that she was on the right track. And she was not alone. Her sisters were here with her and together they walked the straight path. 'Brothers' sat in the male prison next door. They would all do their 'time' within the hot dung-heap of Egypt's punishment block. And out of that fertile incubating ground would rise a new Egypt. It would be an Egypt faithful to the Lord, submitted, truly Muslim....

Khadija's musings were cut short in midstream by the sound of heavy footfalls. A darted glance through the bars to the open courtyard beyond stirred her limbs into action. Sprinting along the corridor between the rows of cell bunks, Khadija proclaimed in hoarse whisper, 'The Director of Public Prosecutions and the Prison Governor are coming!'

A flurry of veils, gloves and headdresses stirred the dust in the cell and turned the beam of light from the high window into a kaleidoscope of shadowed comings and goings. Within seconds, the sisters were sat, carefully cloth-covered, steeling themselves for the male intrusion with its usual harangue and pointed innuendos.

Certainly they felt frightened; after all where were their male protectors? Equally, however, they felt that they were the victors, enduring something rather like the death rattle of a system that had long since grown paralysed with the poison of apostasy. Theirs, with a little more waiting, would be the revival, the dawn, the Islam intended by God.

CHAPTER TWELVE

A PASSIONATE AFFAIR

Together or apart?

EGYPT HAS PLAYED HOST to the most prominent Islamic reformist movement in Sunnî Islam over the last sixty years. The relationship between successive governments and the Muslim Brotherhood (*Al-Ikhwân al-Muslimûn*) has meandered across the spectrum from open support to utterly opposed.

Figure 13
Emblem of Al-Ikhwân Al-Muslimûn

For most of the time the authorities in Egypt have viewed the activities of the Brotherhood with deep suspicion. A wavelike pattern emerges as one traces the history of the relationship. When, for whatever reason, a government lifts its restrictions upon the Brotherhood's activity, the latter takes giant strides forward in publicising and pursuing its goals. The government then feels obliged to clamp down even harder. Political changes, or circumstances beyond the government's control, urge a softening of attitude towards the Brotherhood. The official courting of the reformist camp gains momentum and the process begins again.

In the 1940s the Muslim Brotherhood was bitterly opposed to the secular, liberal-constitutional parties, especially the Wafd Party. Sometimes the Brotherhood flirted with the king against the elected Wafd government. In 1948, when the then Prime Minister proclaimed martial law and banned the Brotherhood, one of its members assassinated him. Hasan al-Banna, founder-leader of the Brotherhood, was killed in retaliation within weeks.

A coup d'état occurred in Egypt in 1952, organised by the Free Officers movement. The king was deposed. The officers had good relations with the Brotherhood, which joined with the rest of Egypt in celebrating the dawn of a new era. At first the Society enjoyed favoured status with the new regime. Twenty-nine months later, six of the Society's members died on the gallows and the organisation was destroyed almost beyond repair. The relationship had soured after Nasser took over as President in 1954.

For many of the Brotherhood's members, the 1950s and 1960s were years of exile or imprisonment. A story was told in those days, illustrating the extreme hostility which marked government/Brotherhood relations:

Nasser missed his fountain pen and reported the loss to the minister of the interior. In a short while the pen was found only to have been mislaid and Nasser called to report again to the minister of the interior. Incredulously, the minister replied,

'How could that be? I have already arrested a number of Brothers who have confessed to stealing your pen.'27

Nasser's death in 1970 and the rise to presidency of Muḥammad Anwar al-Sâdât (Sadat) led to a new courtship between government and reformist Muslims in Egypt. Sadat released all Brotherhood prisoners, came up with the slogan 'Faith and Science' and cultivated an image of himself as 'The Believer President'.

Sadat wanted to oust the left-leaning group in the ruling Arab Socialist Union and ordered the establishment of Islamic Associations in universities and factories. The avowed aim was the combatting of atheistic Marxism. Brothers returned from exile in Saudi Arabia and elsewhere and assumed a higher profile in Egyptian political and national life.

Soon, Sadat realised that he had unleashed a lion. More radical groups split away from the original Brotherhood. These clandestine cells sought immediate reform by armed struggle. The Islamic Liberation Group, for example, mounted an armed attack on the Technical Military Academy in Cairo in 1974. Its aim was to capture the Academy's armoury and then march on the ruling party's headquarters in central Cairo where the President was due to give a speech. It would there overthrow the regime and establish an Islamic estate. Thirty soldiers lost their lives before the Islamists were stopped. The government had to stamp down on all 'extremists'.

Over the next years Sadat's relationship with the Muslim Brotherhood followed a pattern of 'now legal, now secret'. A politicising of the movement took place during the late 1970s, with Brothers obtaining a strong voice in the People's Assembly. The Muslim Brotherhood remains a significant political force in Egypt.

At the same time, a plethora of secret organisations engaged the loyalties of those Muslims for whom the political route spelled only delay and compromise. The activities of such groups have burst sporadically to the surface of Egyptian society precipitating extreme measures by the authorities in their efforts to uproot and suppress them.

Figure 14 illustrates the vagaries of the relationship between the Egyptian authorities and the reformist Muslims (Islamists) over the last half-century.

Figure 14
The Islamists in Egypt 1940–1990

Date	The Brotherhood and Successors	Relationship with the Authorities	Significant Events
1940	500 branches.		
1941		Al-Banna banished to Upper Egypt on British orders.	
1946	300,000 active members.	Government encourages Brotherhood in its struggle against Wafd Party and communists.	
1948	'Secret apparatus' assassinates a judge.	Brotherhood banned.	December: Prime Minister Nuqrashi Pasha imposes martial law; three weeks later assassinated.
1949	2,000 branches and 0.5 million active members.	Hasan al-Banna killed.	
1950		Ban lifted.	Martial law lifted.
1951	Hudaybi becomes Supreme Guide of Brotherhood.		

Date	The Brotherhood and Successors	Relationship with the Authorities	Significant Events
1952	Brotherhood plays significant role in riots.		January: widespread riots. Monarchy shaken.
		Brotherhood exempt. Neguib visits Banna's tomb to pay respects.	23 July coup; Neguib and Nasser ban all political parties.
1953	1,500 branches. Secret cells revived to carry out assassinations, without approval of Hudaybi.	Nasser's reforms opposed by Brotherhood as unIslamic.	Nasser replaces Neguib; begins implementing land reform.
1954		Rauf and five others executed, 4,000+ jailed. Severe torture.	23 October Abdul Munim Abdul Rauf tries to kill Nasser at a rally in Alexandria; fails.
1957		21 Brothers slaughtered in Tura prison.	
1962	Unification of various groups around neo-Brotherhood. Readings of Qutb's book *Signposts*.		

Date	The Brotherhood and Successors	Relationship with the Authorities	Significant Events
1964		Brotherhood members released, including Qutb. Brotherhood leaders implicated; 1,000 arrested, 365 tried.	General amnesty. Three assassination plots uncovered.
1965		Further repression.	Nasser, in Moscow, denounces a new conspiracy by Brotherhood.
1966		Top leaders (including Qutb) executed.	
1967	Formation in prison camps of Islamist groups alienated from Egyptian society.		War versus Israel and defeat of Arabs; sympathy with Brothers' diagnosis of ills of Egyptian Muslim community.
1970		Release of all Brotherhood prisoners.	Nasser dies; Sadat rules: 'The Believer President'.
1971		Brotherhood exiles return from Saudi Arabia.	Corrective action versus leftists; Sadat directs establishment of 1,000 Islamic Associations in universities and factories.

Date	The Brotherhood and Successors	Relationship with the Authorities	Significant Events
1973	Growth of the radical *Jamâ'at Islamîya* (Islamic Associations).	Regime encourages the *Jamâ'at Islamîya*.	'Successful' October war fought versus Israel on Islamic slogans.
1974		Punishment of offenders.	Islamic Liberation Group's attack on Technical Military Academy to obtain arms to overthrow Sadat in Cairo; fails.
1975	Neo-Brotherhood emerges as a political force.	Reintegration into Al-Azhar University.	General amnesty declared by Sadat.
1976	More militant Brothers develop strong, secret groups: *Jamâ'at al-Muslimûn* (Society of the Muslims) popularly known as *Al-Takfir wa'l-Hijra* (The Denunciation and the Migration); *Munazzamat al-Jihâd* (The Jihad Organisation); and others.	Brothers stand as independents or members of the ruling party. Monthly *Al-Da'wa* published again. The *Jamâ'at Islamîya* control the congress of the Student Union.	Return to multi-party system.

Date	The Brotherhood and Successors	Relationship with the Authorities	Significant Events
1977	January: members of *Al-Takfir wa'l-Hijra* play major part led by Shukri Ahmad Mustafa. Previously living in caves in Minya. Official investigation reveals that the organisation has 3-5,000 members.	Security forces arrest 60 members. Younger members demand trial or release of Mustafa and others; not granted. 3 July they kidnap and kill former Waqf minister Sheikh al-Dhahabi. 620 members arrested and 465 tried by military courts. 5, including Mustafa, are executed.	Burning of nightclubs during 3 days of widespread rioting caused by withdrawal of government subsidies on bread, etc. Sadat's seeking of peace with the Israelis is unpopular.
1978	Brotherhood and offshoots gain control of 60% plus nearly all Islamic Associations.	Regime robs the *Jamâ'at Islamîya* of their success in student elections.	Spring elections for student union officials.
1979	Brotherhood heavily involved.	September: Sadat jails 2,000 dissidents and shuts down *Al-Da'wa*. Military purged of 200 officers; 4,000 privately-run mosques to register with ministry.	Signing of peace treaty. In August over 100,000 gather for prayers outside presidential palace; shout anti-Sadat slogans.

Date	The Brotherhood and Successors	Relationship with the Authorities	Significant Events
1980			Violent incidents between Copts and Islamists in Asyut.
1981	Instigated by *Al-Jihâd* members.	September: Sadat jails 1,500+ Islamists including Muhammad al-Islambuli; demotes Coptic Patriarch.	June: anti-Coptic riots in neighbourhood of Zawîya al-Hamra', Cairo.
	Assassination led by Khalid Ahmad Shawki Islambuli. He and his colleagues belong to *Munazzamat al-Jihâd*, directed by Muhammad Abdul Salam Faraj (ideologist), Sheikh Umar Abdul Rahman (a blind professor at Asyut University) and Abbud Abdul Latif Zumur (Lieutenant Colonel, military intelligence).	In October Mubarak imprisons 3,000+ extremists belonging to *Al-Jihâd*.

Interior Minister Abu Basha has Islambuli and colleagues executed (including Faraj). | 6 October: 4 soldiers armed with automatic weapons attack review stand at military parade killing Sadat and 7 others. Insurrection in Asyut. Husni Mubarak takes over as President. |

Date	The Brotherhood and Successors	Relationship with the Authorities	Significant Events
1982		140 Islamic militants arrested. Government steps up infiltration of fundamentalist groups. Mubarak uses Al-Azhar ʿulamâ to re-educate jailed Islamist extremists.	More open political process leads to combining of opposition elements in parliament and Islamic elements outside to demand full sharîʿa application immediately.
1983		Second trial of Al-Jihâd group.	
1985	Islamists dominate the syndicates of doctors, journalists, lawyers, and engineers. Funded by 7 huge Islamic holding companies, financed by Egyptians working in Gulf and popular with small Islamist investors: gives strong economic base.	Pro-sharîʿa marches and demonstrations banned. Car stickers banned. Rights of students to organise curtailed.	

Date	The Brotherhood and Successors	Relationship with the Authorities	Significant Events
1986	Islamist groups involved.	30 army members arrested for setting up combat training centres with a view to overthrowing the government.	February: 17,000 conscripts of the Central Security Police riot in 5 provinces, including Cairo. Largescale destruction of symbols of wealth and Westernisation.
1987			April: parliamentary election; Muslim Brotherhood allies with Liberals and Socialist Labour Party under slogan 'Islam—that is the solution'. 36 Muslim Brotherhood members in new chamber dominate the Alliance's activity, demanding immediate application of sharī'a, promotion of Islamic investment companies, termination of Egypt's strategic and economic links with the USA and abrogation of the Camp David peace process.
	Total membership of all groups estimated at 70-100,000.		

Beyond the Brotherhood

The 1970s saw the formation of Islamist groups whose members were too young to have participated in the anti-colonial struggle. The new radicals were almost all urban-based and many of them were students and graduates. They saw the success of the 1973 war, fought under a Muslim slogan, as a model of what could be achieved when *jihâd* (holy war) was properly undertaken. In their view, the 1973 war was simply directed at the wrong enemy. The prime enemy lived closer to home. It was this internal opponent who procrastinated in applying Islamic law (the *sharî'a*) and who encouraged the neglect of proper Islam. The political, economic and religious leadership of the country revelled, unchecked, in terrible apostasy.

Several organisations challenged the leaders of Egypt during the decade. The 'Military Academy' cell gained its nickname from the failed coup d'état attempt in 1974, centred on the Military Academy in Cairo. This armed attack was mounted by the Islamic Liberation Organisation under the leadership of Salah Siriya. The Society of Muslims (*Jamâ'at al-Muslimûn*) was nicknamed 'The Denunciation and the Migration' (*Al-Takfir wa'l-Hijra*) by the government. This group played a major role in the rioting in Cairo in early 1977. Shukri Ahmad Mustafa led its operations until his capture and execution. In the summer of 1977 followers of Mustafa kidnapped and assassinated the Minister of Religious Foundations. The Jihad Organisation (*Munazzamat al-Jihâd*), some of whose members assassinated Sadat in October 1981, was instrumental in the severe anti-Coptic riots during June of that year.

The founders and central members of these major militant groups had been badly tortured while imprisoned under Nasser. Their ideological views were strongly inspired by the writings of Sayyid Qutb. They differed from one another in some of their emphases, for example, as to whether it is all Egyptian Muslims who are in effect 'unbelievers' living in a *jâhilî* ('ignorant') society or whether it is just their rulers. They functioned quite independently and frequently condemned one another as falling short of the true ideal. They all clashed violently with the government as Figure 15 illustrates.

Group	Clash	Leader/ Ideologue	Executed
The Muslim Brotherhood *Al-Ikhwân al-Muslimûn*	Plotted overthrow of Nasser	Sayyid Qutb	1966
Islamic Liberation *Tahrir Islâmî*	Attempted coup against Sadat	Salah Siriya	1975
Society of Muslims *Jamâ'at al-Muslimûn*; The Denunciation and the Migration *Al-Takfir wa'l-Hijra*	Anti-government riots in Cairo; murder of Sheikh al-Dhahabi	Shukri Ahmad Mustafa	1978
Jihad Organisation *Munazzamat al-Jihâd*	Anti-Copt riots; assassination of Sadat	'Abd al-Salam Faraj	1982

Figure 15
Islamists and government: fight to the death

In the eyes of the Islamists of the 1970s, President Sadat came across as far from being 'the Believer President'. The Camp David peace treaty with Israel, plus the celebratory Carter-hugs of Sadat's wife, Jihan, were the last straw for the radical reformists. On 6 October 1981, an officer and three soldiers stormed the review stand at a military parade in Cairo. Sadat and seven others, including a well-loved Coptic bishop, were killed.

The soldiers were led in their mission by twenty-four-year-old Lieutenant Khalid Ahmad Shawki Islambuli. The Jihad

Organisation to which Islambuli belonged was directed by a young Islamic ideologist named Muḥammad ʿAbd al-Salâm Faraj. When it came to punishment for the assassins of President Sadat, the uniformed men who fired the automatic weapons were executed, plus Faraj.

More *jihâd*

Faraj was the author of a pamphlet which was refuted point by point by none less than the Mufti of Egypt in a national newspaper two months after Sadat's death. Faraj's work expresses the ideology behind the militancy of the men who saw Sadat as standing in the way of God's will for Egypt.

The title of Faraj's work is *The Neglected Duty, Al-Farîḍa al-Ghâ'iba*.[28] It begins by quoting the Qur'ân:

Has not the time arrived
For the Believers that
Their hearts in all humility
Should engage in the remembrance
of God and of the Truth
Which has been revealed (to them),
And that they should not
Become like those to whom
Was given Revelation aforetime,
But long ages passed over them
And their hearts are hard?
For many among them
Are rebellious transgressors (sura 57:16).

The duty that has been neglected is, of course, *jihâd*. Faraj aims to stir his audience to an armed struggle against the rebellious transgressors in contemporary Egyptian society. Although Sadat is never mentioned by name in the text of the pamphlet it is obvious that his regime constitutes the current infidel or apostate state against which *jihâd* must be waged.

No other way

Faraj's constant theme is that the contemporary 'spiritual' health of Muslims in Egypt is far from what God would have it to be.

Those seeking to bring about a positive change in that state of health are going about it in the wrong way, according to Faraj. The benevolent societies, of which there are thousands in Egypt, may do a lot of good work in the short term but do they bring about the foundation of an Islamic state? The Sufi movement may assist many Egyptian Muslims with growing in personal piety but by doing so they help too many Egyptians miss the wood for the trees: the common goal has to be, not more piety, but obedience to God's Word—bringing in the rule of God.

The Muslim Brotherhood and other reformists aim to achieve some good by exerting pressure as a political party. Faraj suggests that all political parties collaborate to some extent with the state in which they are active. Some Egyptian Muslims proceed by infiltrating the government apparatus and changing things from within. Perhaps the author has in mind here Shaykh Al-Sha'râwî, a popular religious leader with a strong TV following who climbed to being a Cabinet Minister in the late 1970s. An infiltrator, however, still has to support the status quo and that would exclude him from being in a position to deny the status quo and inaugurate something totally different.

What about those fellow reformists who withdraw from *jâhilî* society and form their own, faithful 'group of separation' that lives out of the way of others, in caves, in a true Islamic setting? Faraj asks how that procedure can bring into reality an Islamic state.

Faraj looks round the contemporary Islamic scene in Egypt and says that all these routes for reform miss the essential method, authenticated by God himself.

Liberation by arms and faith

The only way to bring about an Islamic state is for a small
minority of Muslims to become radically committed to *jihâd*
in the sense of armed struggle. The Qur'ânic promise is that
if only the true Muslims will take the initiative and obey
God's command to *jihâd*, then as they open fire on the
unbelievers God himself will intervene on their behalf and
change everything:

> Fight them, and God will
> Punish them by your hands,
> Cover them with shame,
> Help you (to victory) over them... (sura 9:14).

The establishment of an Islamic state is obedience to a
command from God. Therefore it is God who is responsible
for working out the details of that establishment as the true
Muslims begin to obey him.

Faraj also deals in detail with military tactics, explaining
the methodology advocated in the Qur'ân and prophetic
example (*sunna*). After all, the faith-fighting has to be done
in the prescribed manner in order for God to lend to it his
authority.

Whether Faraj's assumption was that, upon the death of
the apostate Sadat, God himself would intervene with a
stupendous miracle or whether the people would rise up
against the regime, recognising the hand of God in the
overthrow of Sadat, it is hard to determine. Certainly the cell
group made no widespread plans for how they were to proceed with the bringing in of an Islamic state. Their assurance
was that their obedience in the first step would lead to the
defeat of the apostate Egyptian leadership and propel them
on to the next step, that of confronting the external infidel—
the non-Muslim world at large.

The Neglected Duty lays out the radical worldview of
Sunnî reformist Muslims in a clear and precise way. As it

proceeds, it also interacts with other radical and non-radical constituents of contemporary Egyptian Muslim society.

Faraj models his work on Qutb's hero, the orthodox theologian Ibn Taimîya. His major point is that Sadat's regime is similar to the rule of the Mongols in the thirteenth and fourteenth centuries. Ibn Taimîya had justified an all-out attack upon the Muslim Mongols by the Muslim Mamluks of his day. The basis of his argument was that the Mongols were apostate Muslims. Every group of Muslims that transgresses Islamic law must be combatted, even though they continue to profess Islam. So said the great theologian. Faraj says that Ibn Taimîya's legal opinion (*fatwâ*) concerning the Mongols authorises a similar dealing with Egypt's contemporary 'Mongol' ruler, Anwar al-Sâdât.

The name of the reformist game has moved a long way from long-term educational efforts. The Islamists' obligation is quite plainly the violent seizure of power.

The worldview of the radical Islamist visionary is self-justifying. It all makes sense, if you accept to look at history and life like that. In the Egypt of President Mubarak and elsewhere in the Sunnî Muslim world, the kind of ideologising and action represented by the Jihad Organisation is not something that will disappear by being ignored or partially accommodated, nor vanish if strongly repressed. It is a worldview accepted more or less by many Muslims. It provides an 'Islamic' way of combatting the continuing economic, political and cultural imperialism of Western nations. It clearly identifies the infidels and apostates at home and abroad. A reformist Muslim can tell you quickly where in the world exists the party of Satan and where the party of God.

CHAPTER THIRTEEN

PEOPLE'S DARLING

An English enigma

HIS NAME WAS ʿALĪ SHARIʾATI (Ali Shariati). There was no big media attention surrounding his coming to England in 1977. Neither was there much interest in his death on 19 June during his visit—at least, not in England.

In Iran, however, people were very angry! SAVAK, as the Shah's secret police force was called, was implicated in Shariati's mysterious death while overseas. Even if SAVAK was not actually involved, ordinary Iranians believed it was. Ali Shariati was one of their popular teachers and inspirers in the years up to revolution. Now the Shah had had him silenced.

Birth of an Islamic sociologist

Ali Shariati was born in Mazinan, a village near the desert in northeast Iran. The year was 1933. He was educated in Mashhad, strongly influenced by the ideas of his father, a dedicated Muslim who established a centre for the spread of Islamic teachings. The older Shariati's concern was to bring the modern-educated youth back to the Islamic fold.

After high school and teachers' training college, Ali Shariati taught while he pursued his studies at the Faculty of Letters in the University of Mashhad. During those years he also married a student companion and served his first prison term. In 1960 he was offered the opportunity to embark on graduate studies at the University of Paris. A remarkable maturing occurred as Shariati got to grips with the analytical and critical school of French sociology. He emerged from his doctoral studies with a strong understanding of the Western sociological approaches to analysing society. He also emerged with a deep conviction that Western models were totally inappropriate for coming to terms with a culture that was rooted in Islam.

Shariati returned to his native land in 1964 where he was immediately arrested and imprisoned for half a year: he had taken part in anti-government activities in France! After a difficult search for employment in the education department, he finally secured a teaching position in history at the University of Mashhad. Very quickly, Shariati became the most popular teacher at the university, much to the chagrin of the university administration. The institution was headed by pro-monarchy men who found Shariati's rigorous and radical approach far too threatening.

Reaching the people

During those early years back in Iran, Shariati frequently travelled to Tehran to give lectures. The trips led to the formation in the capital of the Ḥusaynîya-i Irshad in 1965. This centre for religious education was deliberately named to recall the celebrated struggle of *Imâm* Ḥusayn against the oppressive domination of Ummayad rule (AD 660–750). The *Imâm* had, of course, been martyred and *ḥusaynîyas* existed in most Iranian towns as focal points of annual remembrances of Ḥusayn's martyrdom. In Iran as a whole, therefore, there has consistently been a strong element of the positive force of martyrdom, especially in the struggle for common justice against oppressive rulers. The naming of Shariati's teaching centre in Tehran was pointed. From there, Shariati's lectures were recorded and diffused by mimeograph.

In his lecturing, both in Mashhad and Tehran, Shariati developed and announced his sociological interpretation of Islam. That interpretation had a cumulative and strong political impact on Iranian society. Eventually the authorities arrested Shariati in the summer of 1973. The functions of the Ḥusaynîya-i Irshad were stopped. Two years later Shariati was released but confined to Mazinan, his birthplace. Tapes of his lectures, however, spread like wildfire throughout Iran. Permission was finally given for him to travel to Europe in the summer of 1977. Shariati went westwards to an enigmatic death.

Putting the world to rights

Shariati's interpretation of Islam appealed to the youth. He spoke with an authoritative understanding of Western intellectual sources and yet he found them wanting. His concern was to evolve a faithful, yet politically challenging, approach to Qur'ânic exegesis. He wanted to provoke Iranians to 'see' things differently and then act because they 'saw'. He was not concerned for traditional Islamic studies but rather for an application of Islam to the needs of contemporary Iranian society.

Shariati proclaimed the spiritual bankruptcy of what the West offered in its humanism, whether of capitalist or Marxist variety. In a lecture entitled 'Humanity between Marxism and Religion', he says:

> We are clearly standing on the frontier between two eras—one where both Western civilization and communist ideology have failed to liberate humanity, drawing it instead into disaster and

causing the new spirit to recoil in disillusionment; and one where humanity in search of deliverance will try a new road and take a new direction, and will liberate its essential nature. Over this dark and dispirited world, it will set a holy lamp like a new sun; by its light, the man alienated from himself will perceive anew his primordial nature, rediscover himself, and see clearly the path of salvation.[29]

Islam is, of course, the major protagonist in this renewal of humanity. Islam alone has a worldview of *tawḥîd*, of wholeness. In true Islam, all of life is viewed primarily from a spiritual standpoint. In such a worldview lies the only hopeful starting point for lasting renewal. Islam has, moreover, a mandate from God to bring liberation to the whole of creation. All humanity needs to be brought into the light of its holistic and religious outlook on life.

Islam alone has a proper view of man, or 'Adam', as both a created being and also a deputy or viceregent, acting on God's behalf in the earth. So man must learn to listen and learn to act. The details of earthly reality are not irrelevant to God; he has a will to be put into practice in every situation.

Shariati saw as a major task the freeing of Islam from the effects of centuries of stagnation, superstition and contamination. He sought to provide the intellectual stimulus for Muslims to take centre stage in the world once again:

This is no extravagant proposal; it is a duty. Not only does the essential summons of Islam require it, but the text of the Qur'an explicitly enjoins it upon the true followers of Islam: 'God is the East and the West. And thus We have made you a middle people, that you might be witnesses to the people, and the Prophet a witness to you' (2:143).[30]

Back to the original

Shariati sought a return to early Shî'ism, the system that existed before the Ummayads plunged Islam into decadence and tyranny. He contrasted that earlier 'Alid Shî'ism' (from 'Alî, the son-in-law of Prophet Muhammad and the first Imâm) with 'Safavid Shî'ism' (from the Safavids, whose Persian Empire existed from AD 1499 to 1736). It was a comparison between pure, original Islam and the diluted, institutionalised Islam of the Safavids. In Shariati's view, the Safavid type of Islam was inherited and embellished by the Pahlavis. It became, under them, an instrument of political enslavement *par excellence*. The main points of Shariati's comparison are summarised in Figure 16.[31]

By his exegesis of the positive qualities of 'Alid Shî'ism', Shariati dissociated himself from the institutionalised, official Islam hated by idealistic Iranians, especially the youth. He also infused original Shî'a concepts with new meaning and force. So, for example, 'prayer' carried political overtones in his vocabulary, implying action. The annual 'Âsh-ûrâ' ceremonies emphasised the idea of fighting and dying for a just cause rather than simply a commemoration of the martyrdom of Ḥusayn. His approach proved very attractive to significant sections of Iranian society.

A people's revolution

Shariati's target audience comprised the 'followers' of Islam, the masses. In his view, Prophet Muhammad's vindication and authentication came because the masses heeded his words and followed him in exodus (*hijra*). The final sura of the Qur'ân provides a major point of departure for Shariati's philosophy:

Say: I seek refuge
With the Lord
And Cherisher of Mankind (*al-nâs*)

Original 'Alid Shî'ism'	Major Concept	Later 'Safavid Shî'ism'
Authority designated to members of family of Prophet alone, because of their knowledge and purity.	visayat—designation of authority	Government at first designated, then made hereditary, eventually enshrined in race and kinship.
Incarnation of religious ideal in 'superior men' as models for life. People to live pure lives in imitation.	imamate	Appeal to 12 supersaints, as intercessors. Doesn't matter how people live. Grace automatic from Imâms.
Belief in the purity of those spiritually and socially responsible; governments accountable.	'ismat—purity	Only found in the sinless 14 (Muhammad, Fâṭima and 12 Imâms), so other leaders can be dishonest; governments can act how they will.
Offering one's friendship to Ali and following his guidance.	vilayat—governance	Love of Ali alone; the individual feels irresponsible.
Assistance of specialists in practical and juridical problems; those specialists not above evaluation.	taqlîd—emulation	Blind obedience to the 'ulamâ, without evaluating their lives or words.
World is based on justice; society to be just, because God is just.	'adl—justice	Theological problem not touching ordering of society. In this world 'justice' is left to monarchies.
Responsibility of people to take guidance and act according to wishes of Imâm, made known through pious leaders.	gha'ibat—absence	Irresponsibility because the Imâm is absent.
Preparation for reform; expectation of the exploited classes for world revolution.	intizar—expectation	Current corrupt state is a result of divine decree. Status quo is maintained at all costs.

Figure 16
'Alid Shî'ism' and 'Safavid (Pahlavi) Shî'ism' contrasted

The King
Of Mankind (*al-nâs*)
The God
Of Mankind (*al-nâs*),
From the mischief
Of the Whisperer
(Of Evil), who withdraws
(After his whisper)—
(The same) who whispers
Into the hearts of Mankind (*al-nâs*)
Among Jinns
And among Men (*al-nâs*) (sura 114).

For Shariati, the Qur'ânic address is being made to *al-nâs*, the people. The Prophet is sent to *al-nâs*, and it is *al-nâs* who are accountable for their deeds—in short, the whole responsibility for society and history is borne by *al-nâs*. The Qur'ân begins in the name of God and ends in the name of the people.

Shariati longed for, and worked towards, a people, a mass, who would be aware of injustice and alienation, and critical of the manipulative ideologies exported by the West to other nations. He wanted ordinary believers to realise their rich heritage as Muslims and awaken to their responsibility for carrying the Islamic vision of *tawhîd* into reality in an Iran gone wrong. The vanguard of that reinvigorated people was to be the youth: students and other young Muslims.

The distance between Shariati's approach and that of Imam Khomeini will become apparent in the following chapter. Nonetheless, the contribution of Ali Shariati towards the Islamic revolution cannot be overemphasised. He brought into focus for many Iranians in the 1970s the reformative aspect of an 'Islam of the people'. Shariati's lectures and writings took their significant toll on the Shah's regime. It would seem that the Shah's hierarchy admitted as much in their desire to have Shariati removed from the face of the earth.

CHAPTER FOURTEEN

PEACOCK'S MATCH

A name to swear by!

WORDS FROM A MUCH-RECITED ODE to Imam Khomeini depict the strength of allegiance ordinary Iranian Muslims own towards their late spiritual and political Leader. The poem is entitled '*Be Nameto Sogand*' or 'We Swear by Your Name':

> The masses rose like the chest of the Oman Sea
> And they raised their fists like the peak of Alvand Mountain...
> The throne is yours in the whole Islamic world
> From the Nile Valley to the banks of the Shatt al-Arab
> You are the Imam among the ulema...
> Your thought is victorious by the glory of the Quran
> And your name is everlasting, we swear by your name.[32]

Ruhallah Musavi Khomeini was born in September 1902 in the provincial town of Khomein, some eighty-five miles southwest of Tehran. His father was murdered soon after his birth so his mother and an aunt looked after his early upbringing. When he was sixteen both females died. An elder brother then oversaw his education.

The making of a prophet

In 1921, Khomeini went to study the religious sciences under the guidance of Shaykh ʿAbd al-Karîm Ha'iri. When Shaykh Ha'iri moved to Qum to found a theological centre there, Khomeini went with him. Through this association, Khomeini became heir to a vibrant Shîʿa theological tradition which included political activism as well as learning. Qum also became the base of his longstanding challenge to the successive governments of Iran.

Khomeini's fame as writer and teacher grew initially through his contribution in the realms of devotional and mystical literature. As he lectured at Qum in the 1930s, Khomeini mixed topics of an ethical and spiritual nature with analyses of the contemporary 'apostasy' occurring in Iran. He warned that a revolution in the moral and spiritual realm was the only valid starting point for healthy societal change.

It was while Khomeini was first at Qum that the Pahlavi state was established by Riza Khan (father of the Shah overthrown in 1979). The new monarch (entitled Shah) gradually transformed the political structure of the nation into a totalitarian dictatorship. 'Modernisation' was a major goal of the royal autocrat. In his verbal attacks on Riza Shah's policies, Khomeini consistently refused to call him 'Shah' and accused him of failing to govern in a way which would foster Islam.

Khomeini's first public statement of a political nature came in the early 1940s after Muhammad Riza Pahlavi had succeeded his father to the throne. By and large, however, during that decade Khomeini followed the leadership of the theological centre in keeping at arm's length from the wheeling and dealing of everyday political life. There was even some co-operation with the monarchy to maintain law and order in the years after World War II when the spectre of leftist-inspired anarchy raised its face.

From 1953 the Shah established his reputation as an autocratic ruler. A military coup, assisted by the USA and

Britain, had overthrown the nationalist government of Muhammad Mussaddiq. Muhammad Riza Pahlavi was returned to the peacock throne from where he proceeded to suppress any expression of dissent from his political, economic and social reforms. For a further decade Khomeini kept quiet.

Gradually, however, the imperative of speaking out with moral force in a climate of tyranny and 'apostasy' came heavily to weigh on Khomeini. He alone of the major religious scholars of Qum publicly supported the students at the theological centre in their campaign against the opening of off-licences in Qum.

A prophet's reward

A major confrontation between the monarchy and Khomeini occurred in 1963. The Shah had designed a 'White Revolution' which would reshape the whole of Iranian life. Khomeini saw it as a deliberate attempt to subordinate Iran to America. He therefore condemned the steps in a series of sermons in Qum. The Shah's regime sent in paratroopers, killing some students. Khomeini shouted vehemently against the regime on the fortieth-day remembrance of the killings. After a further denunciation of the Shah's tyranny and 'apostasy' on the tenth day of Muḥarram, the most emotionally intense day of the religious calendar for Shî'a Muslims, the Shah had had enough. He had heard too many declarations from the prophet of Qum. The latest outburst angered him considerably:

> I advise you Mr Shah. Shah sir, I advise you to change your ways. If one day your masters decide you should go, I would not want the people to have cause to celebrate your departure. I do not wish for you the same destiny as your father.... God knows that the people rejoiced when Pahlavi left.... Listen to the advice of the clergy.... Do not listen to Israel.... I hope when you said that the reactionaries are impure animals, you were not

referring to the clergy. Otherwise our duty will be most onerous and you will have a difficult time. You will not be able to live. The people will not let you continue. Are Islam and the clergy black reactionaries? But you black reactionary, you have created this white revolution. For what is this white revolution?[33]

The morning after delivering these words, Khomeini was arrested. Immediately, thousands of people in towns all over Iran protested. They were met with military might and many were killed. The government claimed that 200 died but the Islamic leaders put the number of dead at over 15,000. For the rest of the world this was 5 June: for Iranians it was the 15th of Khurdad, a day they would never forget.

The following year Khomeini was sent into exile in Turkey and then to Iraq. He was permitted to settle in Najaf, one of the Shīʿa shrine cities in that country. For the next thirteen years, from Najaf, Khomeini commented and preached, lectured and wrote about the situation in Iran.

Gradually the climate inside Iran reached fever pitch. At the end of 1977, Khomeini's son was assassinated in Iraq and the following year Khomeini himself was expelled. He moved to France. In many ways, as the stakes in Iran's future became higher, much hinged for the ordinary people around the regime's attitude to their Imam Khomeini.

An end and a beginning

At one point in 1978 the government-controlled press in Iran attacked Khomeini as an agent of foreign powers. It was an ill-timed provocation. The following day in Qum there were public demonstrations which were suppressed only with heavy loss of life. Those demonstrations marked the beginning of the end for the royal family. A series of popular marches and gatherings unfurled across the nation reaching massive proportions in the special month of Muharram. Muharram is the holy month in which Shīʿa Muslims recall the martyrdom of Husayn, and in 1978 it coincided with

December. The Shah finally left Iran on 16 January 1979 and Imam Khomeini returned home on 1 February. Ten days later came the Day of Revolution when armed civilians brought down the puppet government left in place by the fleeing monarch.

For Khomeini himself it is 1 April 1979 which is the special date:

> This day of Farvardin 12, the first day of God's government, is to be one of our foremost religious and national festivals; the people must celebrate this day and keep its remembrance alive, for it is the day on which the battlements of the twenty-five hundred-year old fortress of tyrannical government crumbled, a satanic power departed forever, and the government of the oppressed—which is the government of God—was established in its place.[34]

The blueprint

In a series of lectures given at Najaf in early 1970, Khomeini had developed his idea of what it means for God to govern. The lectures were later published as *Islamic Government (Hukumat-i Islami)*.

Khomeini was addressing students of the religious sciences and he saw in his hearers people who would one day assume positions of influence in Iranian Muslim society. He wanted to prepare them for delivering the proper goods when the time came.

The primary focus of the lectures stresses the need to subordinate political power to Islamic goals and worldview:

> Islamic government does not correspond to any of the existing forms of government. For example, it is not a tyranny, where the head of state can deal arbitrarily with the property and lives of the people, making use of them as he wills, putting to death anyone he wishes, and enriching anyone he wishes by granting landed estates and distributing the property and holdings of the

people. The Most Noble Messenger (peace be upon him), the Commander of the Faithful (peace be upon him), and the other caliphs did not have such [powers]. Islamic government is neither tyrannical nor absolute, but constitutional. It is not constitutional in the current sense of the word, ie, based on the approval of laws in accordance with the opinion of the majority. It is constitutional in the sense that the rulers are subject to a certain set of conditions in governing and administering the country, conditions that are set forth in the Noble Qur'an and the Sunna of the Most Noble Messenger. It is the laws and ordinances of Islam comprising this set of conditions that must be observed and practised. Islamic government may therefore be defined as the rule of divine law over men.[35]

Islamic law (*sharî'a*) is therefore to be the order of the day. As a consequence, only those who are expert in the understanding and interpretation of that law should be overseers of the inauguration of Islamic rule. Experts in *sharî'a* law are alone the qualified people to bring into existence the government of God. They also need to be the people who watch over its functioning. The jurists or *fuqahâ'*, theologians expert in the handling of the law, have to be the ones to assume governance.

Khomeini summed up this contention in a single phrase. In the new Iran it will be a case of *vilayat-i faqîh*, governance by the expert in Islamic law:

The entire system of government and administration, together with the necessary laws, lies ready for you. If the administration of the country calls for taxes, Islam has made the necessary provision; and if laws are needed, Islam has established them all. There is no need for you after establishing a government, to sit down and draw up laws, or, like rulers who worship foreigners and are infatuated with the West, run after others to borrow their laws. Everything is ready and waiting. All that remains is to draw up ministerial programs, and that can be accomplished with the help and cooperation of consultants and advisers who are experts in different fields, gathered together in a consultative assembly.[36]

Qualifications for governing

Khomeini carefully outlined the standards he expected in the lives of those with expertise in understanding sacred law (the *fuqahâ'*). Renewal had to begin at home. Self-reform was essential within the religious establishment. If they were going to administer the affairs of the Muslims in Iran they must be totally disinterested in the world and devoid of worldly ambition. The sheep must be separated from the goats:

> We must improve ourselves spiritually and improve our way of life. We must become more ascetic than before and completely shun the goods of this world.... If your purpose in studying is— God forbid—to secure your future livelihood, you will never become *fuqaha* or trustees of Islam. Prepare yourselves to be of use to Islam; act as the army for the Imam of the Age, in order to be able to serve him in spreading the rule of justice.[37]

Only cleansed and committed 'clergy' would constitute the appropriate vanguard and rearguard for what lay ahead. The work of bringing in the government of God could only be entrusted to those who were themselves totally sold out to that government in their own lives.

Khomeini's Najaf lectures ended in prayer to the God from whom alone is success. From the vantage point of a decade beyond the popular revolution in Iran and the establishing there of an Islamic government, it appears that Khomeini's prayer has been amply answered in the affirmative.

CHAPTER FIFTEEN

THE GREAT SATAN!

'**D**OWN WITH SATAN! DEATH TO THE USA!
Down with Satan! Death to the USA!'
Raihaneh's voice merged with the high-pitched, staccato shrieks of a thousand other women.

'Down with Satan! Death to the USA!'

These closely veiled, chador-shrouded demonstrators had broken away from the main rally to congregate at the former United States embassy in Tehran. The slogan-daubed walls reminded Raihaneh of the months of 'the second revolution'. She remembered the anger outside the compound when it was discovered that documents had been systematically shredded in the early days of the takeover. The involvement of the Americans in the Shah's dirty tyranny was undoubtedly spelled out in those ripped, charred papers. The world of the West had dubbed it 'the hostage crisis'. No! It was a revolution by Iranians who for years had been held hostage to the puppet-Shah's American masters!

Even now, the Americans continued to put their hand into Iran's internal affairs. Who, if not the Great Satan, was behind the present attempts to destabilise the Islamic Republic? Would these infidels never learn that no one can oppose God, not even a so-called 'superpower'?

Raihaneh chanted until she was hoarse.

Eventually the young ladies were persuaded by Revolutionary Guards to disperse to their homes. The shouting had gone on long enough; now it was time to pray and prepare the evening meal for their families.

As Raihaneh walked with her friends towards home in the southern quarters of the busy capital, she joined in the hoarse conversation concerning Iran's enemy number one.

'How can those Western sluts point their finger at us, saying that we are being returned to medieval bondage? We women are secure in the path which the Lord has set out for us.'

'Yes,' interjected Ferri, 'The Qur'ân and *sunna* set us free to be women as we should be. Not like those painted dolls that used to flaunt their Western "freedom" around this city. The ones who knew they were women dressed like prostitutes, showing their pink flesh to every male eye. The others who dressed like men, who behaved like men, "equal this, equal that", they didn't even know that they were women with breasts!'

'Our families will see us securely married! We shall be able to fulfil our religion and produce children for our husbands.'

'Our way is the way of God. Can you imagine a society where a woman takes it upon herself to marry this one today, that one tomorrow?' asked Raihaneh.

'Or just to live with a partner and never marry?' interposed Pari. 'Can you imagine that? If ever a nation need *sharî'a* law it is America!'

'No wonder their menfolk are so lost. They are born of a generation of prostitute mothers! Our Komitehs have cleaned out the red-light sore in our city; there is hope with God for the girls who sold their flesh there. But who can clean out a nation of adulterers?' harangued Raihaneh.

'Our Leader is right when he calls that nation the Great Satan! What a cleansing has taken place here to throw off the choking grip of such unbelievers on our country. God has truly saved us. Thanks to God for our leaders! Thanks to God for the watchful care of the Twelfth *Imâm*! Thanks to God for the martyrs who have shed their blood to set us free! Thanks to God for our holy Imam!'

Wending their way between the fast-moving traffic, the young ladies caught up with friends and neighbours who had stayed with the main rally on the university campus. Conversations gradually shifted from the Great Satan abroad to domestic gossip and friendly reminders to pick up some fruit and bread on the way home.

CHAPTER SIXTEEN

THE GOVERNMENT OF GOD

Detoxification

THE POPULAR REVOLUTION IN IRAN was one thing. What was to replace the Pahlavi regime was another! The ousting of the Shah was preparatory work, not final. The return of Khomeini to Qum was prospect, not panacea. Iranians lived on hope until more than superficialities could be addressed.

Their hero soon spoke out:

> ...our problems and miseries are caused by losing ourselves. In Iran until something has a Western name it is not accepted.... The material woven in our factories must have something in the Latin script in its sleeve edges.... Our writers and intellectuals are also 'Westoxicated' and so are we.... We forget our own phrases and the word itself. Easterners have completely forgotten their honour.... As long as you do not put aside these imitations, you cannot be a human being and independent.[38]

When Imam Khomeini spoke these words the Islamic revolution was more than half a year old. He was speaking as much as an Iranian as a religious leader. Both he and Ali Shariati before him borrowed the language of a much-loved

Iranian polemicist who died ten years before the revolution occurred.

Jalal Al-e Ahmad (1923–1969) had stirred up a lot of controversy in the Shah's time with his thunderings against 'Westitis'.[39] After the revolution his works flooded bookshops and bookstalls throughout Iran. How could Iranians have become so 'plagued by the West', so 'West-struck'?

Imam Khomeini was using Ahmad's words to serve notice that the crisis facing Iran in 1979 was deeper than purely political or economic. It had to do with a deliberate erosion of an Islamic worldview. Khomeini himself appointed and directed leaders of Friday prayers as a force for the reconstruction of a proper worldview, a faithful way of looking out on the whole of life. Iranian Muslims were to be challenged at their Friday midday prayers at every level of existence, for they had lost their way.

Revolutions galore

The reforming of mass consciousness is a huge objective and a long-term one. The restructuring of political and economic life is more tangible and measurable. Within four years of the revolution, a radical transformation of Iranian public life had occurred under Imam Khomeini's tutelage. Figure 17 summarises some of the major steps in the institutionalising of such change.

Three 'revolutions' punctuated the progress of reform. The first occurred as the Shah left Iran for good. The second took place as students invaded the United States embassy in Tehran, holding American diplomats hostage. The third occurred as Bani-Sadr was impeached and removed from presidential office. These 'revolutions', though easily accessible to the mass media, were really the cream on the cake.

The real revolution was going on far more steadily as the Islamic Republican Party gradually consolidated its power. The formal writing into the constitution of the *vilayat-i faqîh*

Figure 17
Timetable for implementing the government of God

Date	Event
1979	
13 January	Khomeini appoints (in exile) an Islamic Revolutionary Council (IRC).
16 January	Riza Shah leaves Iran *(the first revolution)*.
1 February	Khomeini returns to Iran from exile.
5 February	Khomeini appoints Mahdi Bazargan Prime Minister of a provisional Islamic government with orders to change the political system of Iran to an Islamic Republic.
11 February	Day of Revolution: Shahpur Bakhtiar's government (instituted by the Shah before he left Iran) and remnants of royalist court yield to groups of armed civilians, the army command remaining neutral.
early March	Khomeini establishes Mustazafin Foundation to consolidate the properties of 63 members of Pahlavi royal family and assets accumulated by others through illegitimate means and to use the income for the welfare of the *mustazafin* (needy or oppressed).
29/30 March	Referendum on question 'Should Iran be an Islamic Republic?' Voter turnout is 89% with 98.2% saying 'yes'.
1 April	Khomeini declares the first day of the government of God.
end April	First draft of new constitution leaked to press; opposed by Shariatmadari (a senior cleric in Qum) and others including ethnic minorities.
18 June	Second draft fails to satisfy critics, both radical Islamists and secular leftists.
3 August	Election to 73-member Assembly of Experts includes 69 Muslims of whom 45 are clerics (36 of them members of Islamic Republic Party—IRP), and 24 are laymen (11 of them associated with IRP). The IRP has two-thirds majority required to pass individual articles of constitution.
18 August	Introduction of the *vilayat-i faqîh* doctrine produces controversy.

Date	Event
1979 contd	
22 October	Khomeini intervenes and publicly declares that the *vilayat-i faqîh* is not created by Assembly of Experts but ordained by God.
4 November	Takeover of US embassy and diplomats in Tehran by militant students *(the second revolution)*.
15 November	Constitution completed.
2/3 December	Constitution is voted on and wins 99.5% of 15,785,956 votes cast.
1980	
25 January	Abol Hassan Bani-Sadr (lay member of IRC) receives nearly 75% of the popular vote for President.
Spring	Elections to 270-member Majlis (parliament).
May	Office for Propagation of Virtue and Prevention of Sin requests pulling down of red light district of Tehran and 1,000 prostitutes are rehabilitated.
May/June	Over 200 drugs traffickers executed.
June	Cultural Revolution and University Crusade to rid universities of unIslamic ideologies, staff and students.
22 September	Iraq invades Iran.
1981	
January	American hostage crisis is resolved by government of Prime Minister Muhammad Ali Rajai.
20 June	Bani-Sadr impeached and removed from office of president *(the third revolution)*.
July	Majlis passes Islamic Dress Law applicable to all women in Iran.
2 August	Premier Rajai elected President with 88% of popular vote but assassinated in same month by *Mujahedîn-i Khalq*—led by Masoud Rajavi. Government responds by executing 1,000+ people.
September	Hojatalislam Ali Hussein Khamanei wins presidential election.
October	Ali Khamanei's nominee for Prime Minister, Mir Hussein Musavi, is accepted by the Majlis. From now, Musavi's government intensifies purging of government and revolutionary institutions and accelerating the pace of Islamisation.

Date	Event
1982	
February	*Mujahedîn-i Khalq* claims it has assassinated 1,200 religious and political leaders of the regime. Government executes 4,000 guerillas.
Spring	War with Iraq begins to turn in Iran's favour.
April	Anti-republic plot uncovered; led by lay Iranian intellectual who had been active in Islamic anti-Shah movement abroad.
30 May	Cabinet approves plans to bring the existing penal and legal codes, civil law, trade law and registration of documents and land into line with the *shari'a*.
August	Government declares all secular law null and void.
21 September	Majlis passes a law on moral offences.
November	Islamic Revolutionary Guards Corps (IRGC) ministry created.
10 December	82-member Assembly of Experts elected to deal with question of next Leader or Leadership Council.
15 December	Khomeini issues 8-point decree Islamising the judiciary.
mid-December	Gradual opening of universities and colleges with new texts.

doctrine (oversight by the supreme expert in Islamic law) was a major step towards realising Khomeini's ideal of government. Gradually the legislature was reduced to size, the executive and judicial functions overhauled and the universities tamed. The introduction of Islamic law (*shari'a*) as arbiter in all kinds of matters and the concomitant throwing out of all secular law marked a significant consolidating of the new political outlook in the Islamic Republic.

By the end of October 1981, the 'Leader', Imam Khomeini, had brought the new Islamic Republic of Iran to a point where a reformist party was firmly in power. Figure 18 shows the top posts which members of the Islamic Republican Party held at that time.

The strong process of Islamisation of society proceeded apace under such a consolidated leadership. The various mammoth problems facing the government—war, poverty

Office	Holder
President	Hojatalislam Ali Hussein Khamanei
Prime Minister	Mir Hussein Musavi
Majlis-speaker	Hojatalislam Ali Akbar Hashimi-Rafsanjani
Supreme Court Chief	Ayatollah Abdul Karim Musavi-Ardebili

Figure 18
The Islamic Republican party in power

of leadership, dislocation of the economy, and so on—proved unable to dislodge the politicians from their main objective.

Follow my Leader

How has Imam Khomeini himself fitted into the post-revolution world of Iran? The fight over his place and power occurred in the autumn of 1979 and was bound up with the formulating of a new constitution. As far as Khomeini was concerned there was really no debate. His view had been clearly expressed in his earlier lectures from exile on Islamic government. The revolution brought no change in his brief: ultimate leadership was to be entrusted to a pious *faqîh*, to a person like himself. That, of course, was what the people wanted anyway. In the end Khomeini stopped the arguing by publicly declaring that the principle to be adopted, that of *vilayat-i faqîh*, was ordained by God himself.

Article 5 of the constitution enshrined this principle. The context within which the *vilayat-i faqîh* is seen as imperative is described in Iranian Shî'a terms. Due to the concealment of Hazrat Vali Asr (Lord of the Age, the 'hidden' Twelfth Imâm[40]), 'the governance and leadership of the nation devolve upon the just and pious faqih who is acquainted with the circumstances of his age'.[41]

This *faqîh* is to be 'Leader'. As such, he is Commander-in-

Chief of the armed forces and head of the Supreme National Defence Council. He approves presidential candidates and appoints the highest judicial authorities. He also appoints the Islamic jurists on the Council of Guardians whose job is to vet all bills and regulations passed by the Majlis.

The Leader is the standard-bearer and watchdog of public life, guardian of the executive, legislative and judicial functions of government and director of the nation's armed forces.

The Leader has to be both just and pious and also acquainted with the circumstances of his age. Imam Khomeini was a charismatic figure who was widely believed to possess just such qualities. Might it not prove a little difficult to discover a suitable successor? The constitution allowed for a Leader to be provided in the form of a Council in the event that the required qualities could not be found in one individual. It took six years for the first Leader (Imam Khomeini) and those close to him to decide on a man to inherit the mantle. In November 1985, Ayatollah Hussein Ali Montazeri was named Leader-designate. He was later replaced by Ali Khamanei, previously President for some years, now acclaimed as an Ayatollah.

The President's role under the constitution is to implement the terms of the constitution, to order the relations between the legislative, executive and judicial powers and to head the executive power.

One major 'Islamic filter' in the legislative process is provided in the Council of Guardians. This twelve-member Council comprises six just Islamic jurists (selected by the Leader) and six lawyers (elected by the National Consultative Assembly).

Previously, the Shah's men had poked around with the Belgian constitution to come up with something for Iran. Now, a returned Iranian exile has brought into being a government based on Islamic law as interpreted by a just and competent jurist (*faqîh*). The new Iran is deliberately intended to evoke the conditions and principles of the Islam of Muhammad and the Shî'a *Imâms*.

Clergy of the world unite!

In many ways, Khomeini viewed the role of the clergy in pre-revolutionary Iran as Marxism sees the proletariat in a capitalist society. They are to be the confronters and eventually the overthrowers of the corrupt rulers of society. We have seen that Shariati (who became the darling of the *Mujahedîn-i Khalq* group) added a strongly Marxist tinge to his interpretation of the Qur'ân. He was promoting a slightly different motivation for a revolution of the people, aiming to mobilise the younger intellectuals of the 1960s and 1970s with his emphasis on *al-nâs* (the masses) of the Qur'ân.

In Iran, however, the clergy, with their independent economic base and their peculiar influence in keeping alive the particularly Shî'a concept of martyrdom-for-a-cause, became the provocateurs of the revolution. Khomeini saw the clergy as the agents of the revolution. Their role, supremely personified in himself, was crucial in the bringing down of the Shah.

After the establishment of Islamic government in the country, the clergy were to continue to play a significant role, guiding and vetting the administration, making sure that the Republic remained authentically Islamic. Shariati's burdens were eclipsed as the revolution settled down to a reconstruction of the political process à la Khomeini. The *Mujahedîn-i Khalq* group was increasingly and brutally quashed. Thousands (certainly 10,000 by the end of 1982) were executed.

Khomeini's view of the clergy at home coloured his perception of clergy abroad. His anger at the seeming hypocrisy of Christian world leaders came out during the American hostage crisis. Amid the unfolding of that chapter in Iranian relationships with the West, the Pope appealed for the unconditional release of Western hostages. Khomeini replied quite angrily:

> For the fifty years when we gave martyrs, went to prison, and the best men of our nation underwent torture, not a single time did the Pope intervene, or think of intervening in support of this oppressed nation, nor did he try to mediate between them and the oppressors that perchance they would desist from tyranny.[42]

To the six priests who came to minister to the hostages at Christmas Khomeini said more:

> Today, the people of the world are subject to the devilish powers who arrogantly confront the teachings of the prophets and hinder the realization of those teachings. The responsibility lies more heavily on the shoulders of the Christian clergy because most of the great powers are Christian or claim to be Christian. It is the responsibility of the Christian clergy to launch a spiritual battle against those powers who act in opposition to the teachings of the prophets and the teachings of Jesus Christ.... Why do you confine your attempts to guide people within the four walls of the church? First of all you must try to guide the ruling classes. The prophets were appointed to oppose the strong.... Do not allow Christianity to lose its honour and status in the eyes of the masses. Do not allow that the Christian clergy be identified by the people as a supporter of the oppressors.[43]

Khomeini sees the Christian clergy of the West as colluders in oppression. Where in the Western world is there a protest movement of Christian clergy equivalent to his own nation's clerical direction of the Islamic revolution? His 'fundamentalism', like Qutb's, comes in the guise of a theology of liberation.

Christians whose lives are inextricably bound up with the 'Caesars' of the USA, Europe, international finance, weapons of war or oil are compromised contenders for righteousness, in the view of the Moses of Iran. The prophets are silenced in the West, in Khomeini's opinion, because they have sold out to the secular worldview. If the Christians really heard their prophet Jesus, they would say similar things to their governments that Khomeini has been trying to say.

The clergy in the West may have fallen short in their prophetic calling. How well have the Iranian clerics managed since they shifted from being agitators against the Pahlavi regime to upholders of the Islamic Republic?

Perhaps an important undercurrent in the wake of the Islamisation process in Iran in the 1980s stirs around the evidence that 'just' and 'pious' clergy may themselves become oppressors. The liberated may take their 'liberation' too far. Before the Iraqi invasion in September 1980, anti-clerical feeling was increasingly being expressed in various cities of Iran. Khomeini himself had to step in strongly to uphold the right of an individual's privacy in the early years of the revolution. He insisted that people's competence for a position in the new administration be judged on their present circumstances, not by interrogating their relatives concerning their past. The deliberate and massive execution of co-collaborators in the revolution, especially members of the *Mujahedîn-i Khalq*, illustrates the ultimate measures deemed necessary to handle visions differing from that of the new status quo in the country. As many Iranians know to their cost, SAVAK has reappeared as SAVAMA. The title of the secret police force may have changed but its methods remain as oppressive.

Even in the government of God, it seems, things can go badly wrong.

PART 3

CHAPTER SEVENTEEN

THE BOTTOM LINE

All or nothing

IT HAS BECOME CLEAR through the previous chapters that Islam is conceived of by Muslims as far more than just a form of piety. It is not 'religion' in the sense that Westerners mean when they ask 'What religion do you follow?' For Islamic reformists all of life coheres around revelation. They are therefore anxious that the last details of their existence should faithfully reflect the divine command. 'What God wills' is the final authority for their lives. Nearly all Muslims, not just reformists or Islamists, feel this way about their 'faith'.

There is an Arabic word which expresses this sense of a total embrace of law and religion, of liturgy and ethic. The word is *sharîʿa* or 'way'. It conveys the idea of 'the right path'. God's guidelines are given for living aright as God's people in God's world. The word occurs once in the Qur'ân in a revelation coming from the Meccan period. In its context it clearly carries the sense of a pathway wider than the mere performance of formal rites:

Then we put thee
On the (right) Way [*sharîʿa*]

Of Religion: so follow
Thou that (Way),
And follow not the desires
Of those who know not (sura 45:18).

The *sharî'a* is what God commands and what man obeys. It is not worked out by man, but given by God. It determines personal, communal, social, civil, political and devotional life. It defines the parameters of proper *islâm* or 'submission'.

Another word is often used by Muslims to denote the law of God: *fiqh* or 'understanding'. The *fuqahâ'* or jurists are men who 'understand', who draw out in legal terms the implications of the divine will.

Authority in Islam, therefore, has to do with law-deducing and law-enforcing.

We need to ask two questions in this chapter. What are the sources for the activities of the legal experts, the jurists? Who, as a result, wields authority in Muslim communities? Incidentally, we will discover the sense in which 'law' carries a different connotation in Islamic communities from that understood within Western societies.

Law in the making

The Qur'ân is, for all Muslims, the fundamental source for the *sharî'a*. It is the primary expression of the will of God for it is, in itself, God's voice to mankind. Where the Qur'ân expresses a precept clearly, the obligation is clearly absolute.

The example (*sunna*) given in words and deeds by Prophet Muhammad is also seen as normative. Stereotyped records of such sayings and acts are known as Traditions (*hadîth*, properly *ahadîth* in the plural). The Traditions have played a major role in both Muslim law-making and in the spirituality of Islam. The validation of Traditions was carefully addressed during the early centuries of the faith's establishment. Authentication revolves around a reliably recorded chain of transmitters (*isnâd*) who have passed on the sub-stance of a Tradition (*matn*) from one relater to another. The major difference between the Sunnî and Shî'a sects of this level of commitment to authority is expressed in an acceptance of different collections of Traditions.[44].

The Qur'ân and prophetic example (*sunna*) are seen as binding upon all Muslims. Unfortunately, perhaps, not every contingency in life is provided for in the Qur'ân and prophe-tic example. Decisions had to be made in the evolving Mus-lim community for which there was no precedent in these basic sources of guidance. Other principles gradually came into play, and around those other principles various schools of jurisprudence grew up.

One principle was that of the universal accord of scholars living at a given period about a particular issue. This is known as 'consensus' (*ijmâ'*). It comprises the unanimous consensus of the Muslim divines (or *mujtahidûn*). Truth, where not explicit in the Qur'ân or Traditions, is safely discoverable within the qualified community of jurists. The specialists reach a consensus through a process of careful scholarly research (*ijtihâd*). There is considerable diversity of opinion as to what period in the history of Islam marks the end of authoritative consensus-reaching. Does its validity apply only to the Companions of the Prophet or to Muslim divines in every age or to whom?

Four Sunnî schools of law emerged in the eighth and ninth centuries with different interpretations of the limits and safe-guards of consensus and other legal and ritual matters. The Ḥanîfî school is broadminded and likes to appeal to reason and personal judgement. The Mâlikî school stresses an appeal to the principle of general usefulness or the common good. The Shâfi'î school attempts to combine an appeal to the Traditions with consensus and uses the principle of reasoning by analogy. The Ḥanbalî school is the most uncompromising and recognises the validity of only the Qur'ân and the *sunna* in law-making.

The Shî'as again part company with the Sunnîs over the issue of consensus. Instead of trusting the community of professional jurists to achieve a right consensus, the Shî'as rely on their divinely enlightened spiritual leaders to guarantee Islamic truth. Such human Imams, spiritual guides for the people and earthly representatives of the Hidden *Imâm*,[45] are entrusted with the process of working out the will of God for their communities (*ijtihâd*).

Another principle applied to law-making in Sunnî Islam is that of 'analogy' (*qiyâs*). By means of analogy the jurists argued from the intention of some specific rule in the Qur'ân or Traditions. An example of one type of legislating by analogy might be the banning of intoxicating drugs in the twentieth century on the grounds that the Qur'ân forbids the intoxicant wine.

Other principles are found in *istişlâḥ*, or what appears to be in the general interest, *istiḥsân*, or considering a thing to be good, and *istidlâl*, or inferring one thing from another. These principles tend to be specific to only one or two schools of law. They derive from a process of personal interpretation (*ra'y*) of a jurist belonging to the law school concerned. The decisions reached by the use of these principles may be rejected by other jurists of the same or different schools.

Figure 19 summarises the sources of authority in Islam. The Qur'ân, the *sunna* (contained in the Traditions), 'consensus' and 'analogical reasoning' comprise the basic building blocks for Islamic jurisprudence. Those building blocks are themselves guaranteed by God, the Prophet Muhammad, the community or the Hidden *Imâm*, and so on. There is a descending security of 'safeguard' reflected in a decreasing reliance upon the particular source concerned. Thus all jurists acknowledge the authority of the Qur'ân in their law-making, for its guarantor is God himself. Most jurists make use of the Traditions but Sunnî and Shî'a experts will refer to different collections of Traditions. Only some jurists will acknowledge the significance of analogical reasoning. Relatively few jurists will depend upon the process of personal interpretation to provide authoritative guidelines for their people.

Source	Safeguard	Substance
Qur'ân	God	Collated after Muḥammad's death; standardised under 'Uthmân.
Traditions (Ḥadîth)	Muḥammad	Six major books of Sunnî sect. Three major collections of Shî'a sect.
Consensus (Ijmâ')	Community/ Hidden Imâm	Four Sunnî schools of law. Shî'a divines in every age.
Analogy (Qiyâs)	Qur'ân/Traditions/Consensus	Analogical reasoning of legists with regard to the teaching of three former sources.
[Istiṣlâḥ Istiḥsân Istidlâl	Personal interpreter (Mujtahid)	Supported by Ḥanîfî school. Supported by Mâlikî school. Supported by Ḥanîfî school.]

Figure 19
Sources of authority in Islam

God's will

The *sharî'a* ('the Way') constitutes the guidelines for man's *islâm* or 'submission'. God has revealed not so much his character as his will. Man's proper response is to give himself to fulfilling that will.

In Western jurisprudence, an act is either lawful or not. Whether it is decent or indecent, rude or gentlemanly is usually irrelevant. It is illegal in England to drive through a red traffic light: it may or may not be impolite. It is legal to wear no clothes in some public places in California: it may or may not be offensive.

Islamic law looks differently upon human activities. Law is the protector of what is valued in human life and what is

honourable in human relationships. Law and morality therefore add up to the same thing in Islam. To live within the law
is to live morally. To act in an immoral way (for example, by
depriving another person of his wealth or honour or health)
invites heavy penalty.

Arabic Term	Meaning	Example	Legal Implication
farḍ	obligatory	prayer	performance rewarded; omission punished
mandûb	recommended	hospitality	performance rewarded; omission not punished
mubâh	silent/neutral	kindness to animals	actions permitted by silence; ie, sometimes performed and sometimes not performed by the Prophet
makrûh	discouraged	divorce	actions disapproved but not punished
ḥarâm	forbidden	drinking alcohol	actions punishable by law

Figure 20
Human activity according to the Sharî'a

Figure 20 describes the way in which the *sharî'a* looks at
human activities. Value judgements are being made as to

whether a particular action is obligatory, recommended, neutral, discouraged or forbidden. Authority is being brought to bear upon how human deeds are valued, how they seem in God's eyes.

Sharî'a-oriented life is normative life in Islam. In the words of one modern apologist:

> Islamic Law or the *Sharî'ah* embodies the Islamic ideal life. Islam is the complete way of life and *Sharî'ah* is the means to arrive at the ideal life recommended by Islam. *Sharî'ah* enables us to bring our life in line with the will of Allah. It is the process of achieving our goal of life.[46]

Who's who

There is, in Sunnî Islam, no equivalent of an institutionalised Christian 'priesthood'. There is certainly no counterpart to the Roman Catholics' Pope, that is, an individual charged with supervising the maintenance of the faith as it has been received. There is consequently no single spokesman for Muslims generally. The Shî'a perspective is different from the Sunnî one as already suggested. We shall explore that difference more fully in a moment.

In Islam, the will of God is a given. It is the discerning of that will which is important. The people who possess such discernment are those who know the data of revelation, supremely of course the Qur'ân, but also the details of prophetic example (*sunna*). The doctors of sacred law (*'ulamâ'*) comprise the 'knowers'. They are therefore the people who are qualified to give an opinion in legal matters and to take the lead in guiding the people in their obedience to God. In a sense, the doctors of sacred law (the divines, the jurists) form the theocratic focus of Muslim society.

'Ulamâ' is the plural of *'âlim*, meaning 'one who knows' or 'learned'. In the Indo-Pakistan subcontinent the equivalent term is *maulâ* or 'lord' (plural *maulawî*). Since Muhammad's death, it has been only such religious scholars, and specific-

ally the jurist-theologians, who could determine what duties are incumbent on Muslims. These jurists are therefore supervisors of the faith. They are not, however, 'priests' in the sense of mediators between man and God. They are 'deducers', explaining God's perspective on human life and community. Final authority, in the sense of deciding what constitutes the detailed will of God in human submission, falls to such 'law-interpreters'.

The supreme legal adviser (*muftî*) gives responses to questions arising from the application of the (*sharî'a*. His advice guides the judges who administer justice. The appointment of supreme legal adviser and judges is in the hands of the Muslim government of the time and place. The official organisation for legal consultations may choose to invest its authority not in an individual (*muftî*) but in a group. In that case, the group is known as the Body of Legal Advisers (*Dâr al-Fatwâ*).

In traditional Muslim communities, therefore, there tend to be two locuses of supreme authority. On the one hand, the directors of the institutes of Muslim studies or the president of the Muslim university speak on behalf of the jurists ('*ulamâ*'). On the other hand, the supreme judge of the religious tribunals, the grand *muftî*, has the last word in any important dispute concerning the application of the law.

The caliph was (until the end of World War I) the political leader of the Muslim community. He had no special religious authority. He administered the law as given and interpreted. So, for example, the doctors of sacred law established the conditions for instituting a holy war and the caliph carried it out.

Figure 21 illustrates the variety of persons of authority in Islam. Such individuals or groups oversee the interpretation of 'the Way', the implementation of justice, the ordering of society and the renewing of commitment by all the people to God's will.

Person	Area of Responsibility	Source of Authority
jurist-theologian *'ulamâ'*	interpretation of 'the Way' (*sharî'a*)	knowledge of data of revelation
legal adviser *muftî*	implementation of justice	knowledge of data of revelation
caliph *khalîfa*	ordering of society	member of Quraysh tribe (Sunnî)/descended from Prophet (Shî'a)
renewer of religion *muhyî al-dîn*	renewal and revival	recognised by consensus of Sunnî community
Muslim divine *mujtahid*	renewal and revival	recognised by consensus of Shî'a community
Sufi leader *shaykh*	directing the life of the Order (*tarîqa*)	insight (*ma'rifa*) recognised by members of the Order
judge or *qâdî*	administering justice	appointed by state
prayer leader *imâm*	leading prayers and preaching in mosque	appointed by congregation or mosque 'parish'

Figure 21
Persons of authority in Islam

The abandoning of the caliphate at the beginning of the twentieth century and the impingement of Western societies upon traditional Islamic ones muddied the waters considerably. The position of the traditional jurists gave way to the authority of bureaucrats and politicians. A mark of this muddying is demonstrated in Egypt where the jurists have consistently produced legal declarations (*fatwâs*) supporting the policies of whatever government is in office, rather than critiquing those policies from the perspective of the *sharî'a*. Such yielding to the secular authorities of the moment has not been looked kindly upon by the reformist movements of the post-colonial era.

The 'officialness' of the authority of both jurist and judge is dependent upon their upholding of the *sharî'a* as the absolute norm and ideal. Their opinions are authorised by the principle of consensus, the record of previous agreement and the reality of present agreement.

The aim in contemporary Muslim law-approving, especially as espoused by the Islamists, is to enhance a conformity with Islamic tradition. There is no problem in living in the twentieth century for a faithful Muslim. Neither the Qur'ân nor the *sunna* have anything against modernity in itself. The question is *how* does a Muslim live as a faithful Muslim in the twentieth century? What expressions of life in the contemporary world are validly Islamic? What actions uphold or deny the values enumerated in the sources of the *sharî'a*?

The Shî'a community differs considerably from the Sunnîs in one major respect concerning persons of authority. It recognises the spiritual authority of the descendants of the Prophet who guide the community (the *Imâms*) and their current representatives on earth. Those representatives are the directly inspired theologians, people like Imam Khomeini. Such authority figures within Shî'a Islam can speak on behalf of the whole community in a way impossible in the Sunnî context. For this reason, Imam Khomeini managed to produce a legal opinion concerning Salman Rushdie's fate which no single, authoritative Sunnî voice could match. It is quite to be expected within a Shî'a community that a huge demand might develop for such theologians to have a significant say in what goes on in their society or country.

Anyone's guess

The data of revelation are the bedrock of what is normative in Islam. The authority of the interpreters of God's will depends upon their grasp of that data. The retention of the authority of the 'official' interpreters of the *sharî'a* is not dependent upon institutionalisation but upon knowledge. It is not their position within a hierarchy which accords them status, but their expertise in law-deducing and law-making.

Knowledge, however, is free for all. If a Muslim, or a group of Muslims, genuinely believe that God's requirements for life in the modern world are different from what the juridical establishment teaches, no one can deny them their say. Anyone could be a Muslim divine (*mujtahid*), that is, a man of faith who seeks to discern what God's will is today. Indeed, there is a certain expectation among Sunnî Muslims, let alone the Shî'a bias in this direction, that in each century a 'reviver of religion' (*muhyî al-dîn*) will arise whose authority must be recognised.

Reformism or Islamism is therefore to be expected. Someone needs in each age to get to grips with the way in which Muslims should faithfully express their submission to God in contemporary circumstances. It is no use governments stamping on expressions of divergence from the classical legal school simply because the state doesn't like to hear any alternative view. Resurgent Muslims today see as an admission of the bankruptcy of the classical legal school that it so frequently fails to critique the government in power. The status quo is betrayed by its dependence for self-protection on political or military force rather than on an appeal to tradition. The obvious requirement is a return to the proper sources of *sharî'a*. Out come the reformist slogans: 'Back to the Qur'ân and *sunna*!' 'Give us the system (*nizâm*) of Mustafa!'

At the other end of the scale is the recognition that no Muslim can be forced to follow the *sharî'a* completely, although certain duties ought to be performed by every Muslim. More or less, all Muslims do in some respects adhere to the *sharî'a*. It comprises their *islâm*, their submission.

It is difficult for a Western worldview which has reified individualism to understand the cohesive force of this ill-defined yet highly motivating movement towards conformity.

The Western worldview requires some form of organised institutionalisation to keep together a plurality of individuals. How can a religion manage without a 'pope' or a 'priesthood'? How can a society function when ultimate authority is constantly subject to further possible interpretations? How can individuals agree to abide in a submission which is open to evaluation by themselves? Islam knows no institutional organisation equivalent to models familiar in the Western world (apart perhaps from Shî'a Islam in some respects). Its norms can therefore only be enforced indirectly. Such indirect enforcement is done by the ordinary faithful sticking to the tradition. The mass of Muslims (*al-nâs*) themselves maintain a community consensus. The people are also powerholders in Islam.

Every now and then movements erupt out of the community calling for reform or renewal. Those movements demand a strict reimposition of 'internal' standards of conduct and an elimination of the 'foreign' elements which have inveigled their way into the society and corrupted it. The Muslim mass is appealed to: it is the jury. Sometimes the people have said 'yes' to those movements, sometimes they have said 'no'. Either way, their verdict has been authoritative.

CHAPTER EIGHTEEN

TICKETS PLEASE!

'**H**OW CAN YOU SAY THAT, UNCLE?' Cherif deferred politely but angrily to the old man seated at the front of the bus.

'How can you say that we must submit to this government of ours when we all know that its leaders do not care about obeying God's Word?'

In his anger, Cherif was treading precariously near the forbidden area of criticising the government in public. He sensed the danger but passion took control. After all, this was something he felt passionately about!

For months, Cherif had been part of a group who boarded buses at the terminal in Algiers to harangue passengers as they awaited a full complement of travellers. The young men passed out literature and held forth in debate or, preferably, monologue. Sometimes they were thrown off the vehicles almost before they had begun. Sometimes their words were received with considerable sympathy, especially by students returning to their home villages or migrant workers visiting their families in the mountains.

As usual, Cherif unselfconsciously gave vent to his feelings before his captive audience. 'Our fathers fought for the independence of this nation. Men like you, respected uncle, gave their lives to rid us of the heathen French. But today we have a country far worse than when the French ruled here. God has given us fantastic natural wealth. We could be truly independent in spirit as well as in economy. But our leaders will not walk the way of God. They choose rather the way of man!'

The youthful preacher shifted his stance, moving a little further up the bus. He wanted his voice to carry to the back where he noticed a group of students noisily settling down for the journey.

'We are led by infidels! We are bankrolled by unbelievers! We are socialists first and Muslims second! We have left the path of the Prophet and God has forsaken us. Let us return to the pure Islam of Prophet Muhammad, praise be upon him! Let us repent and reject the false prophets who steer our nation deeper into the abyss! Wait! Don't let my words blow over you like the desert wind. This message is not from a mere man. Listen to God:

> Only those are Believers
> Who have believed in God
> And His Apostle, and have
> Never since doubted, but
> Have striven with their
> Belongings and their persons
> In the Cause of God:
> Such are the sincere ones.

'As you well know, those words are from *sûra Ḥujurât*. Now listen to the *sunna*:

> When people are stingy with their money, buy and sell on credit, follow the tails of cattle, and abandon jihâd in God's way, God almighty will inflict a humiliation upon them which He will not lift from them until they go back to their religion.

'The Imam Aḥmad related this in his *Musnad* and so did al-Tabarânî in his *Al-Kabîr*. Our call to true Muslims in

Algeria today is to *jihâd*, the *jihâd* of God! There is a war to be won and the enemies are many.

'Remember God's words, and blessed and almighty is he, about fighting the People of the Book, those Jews and Christians of Prophet Muhammad's own day!

Fight those who believe not
In God nor the Last Day,
Nor hold that forbidden
By God and His Apostle,
Nor acknowledge the Religion
Of Truth (even if they are)
Of the People of the Book,
Until they pay the Jizya
With willing submission,
And feel themselves subdued.

'Today's People of the Book are the Western Zionists! They must be fought on all fronts. They are undoubtedly our enemy!

'But there is another enemy, far worse than the West! Remember what God's Word says about those Muslims who didn't want to go all the way with the Prophet, peace be upon him? Remember the verses?

Those who were left behind
(In the Tabûk expedition)
Rejoiced in their inaction
Behind the back of the Apostle
Of God: they hated to strive
And fight, with their goods
And their persons, in the Cause
Of God: they said,
"Go not forth in the heat."

'What does God say about those apostates?

Let them laugh a little:
Much will they weep:
A recompense for the (evil)
That they do.

'Such people were to be deliberately excluded from the joys of the *umma* when the true society of believers was established. It is related thus in our holy Qur'ân, *Tawba sûra*. Things haven't changed with God. As it was then, so it is today. God curse our apostate leaders!'

Cherif had much more he wanted to declare on the subject of false and true *islâm* but out of the corner of his eye he noticed Bouhedjar tumbling off the bus alongside. Had someone called the security forces? Had Bouhedjar's audience contained a secret policeman, or an army officer in mufti?

With a hurried shout of 'There is no God but God' Cherif dashed off the bus and ran for the safe house he often used when on duty at the crowded terminal.

CHAPTER NINETEEN

POINTS OF VIEW

Fundamentalist indeed?

THERE IS A SENSE IN WHICH ALL MUSLIMS are 'fundamentalist'. They are deliberately literalist in the concept they have of revelation. The Qur'ân is sent down in a specific literary form as God's final Word to mankind. It is mediated by dictation or recitation to and through the Prophet Muhammad. The resultant Word on earth is to be received and obeyed: it conveys God's will. Cherif's harangue on an Algerian bus finds a mostly sympathetic hearing because he speaks from the Book. That book, as all the passengers recognise, *is* the Word. The Arabic composition conveyed to Muhammad constitutes a transcribing of the divine Book in heaven.

The Islamic concept of revelation/inspiration is obviously very different from the biblical picture. In the Bible, God's characteristic manner of revealing his truth is by his word spoken through prophets/witnesses in the events of the biblical history. The prophets/witnesses are active, not passive, participants in that process. They co-operate with the Spirit, acting out and speaking out his in-breathed burden (2 Peter 1:21). The supreme focus of that burden is Christ. The Old Testament is a story about Christ by way of prophecy. The

New Testament is a record about Christ by way of proclamation. One gospel writer sums up the momentum of divine revelation: 'the Word became flesh' and lived on earth among humankind. The Gospels are deemed 'Scripture' because they reliably disclose the Jesus in whom faith is centred. The biblical record is not an end in itself but a channel or witness to the Christ.[47]

Muslims as a whole are 'fundamentalist', by contrast, in that their lives are determined by a text. The text is an end in itself. It declares the way in which man may be truly Muslim, submitted to God. All prophets in the Muslim view are carriers of words from God, not in the sense of the Lord vitalising their spiritual and mental powers, but in the sense of their becoming verbal transmitters of a message from heaven. The Qur'ân is, of course, God's final speech, mediated by Muhammad, the seal of the prophets. A typical confession may take the following form:

> For all Muslims...faith should be an 'all or nothing affair'. The reasons are as decisive as they are simple. One cannot properly embrace the authoritative integrity of a partly fallible scripture. Muslims quite rightly interpret the Koran to be an error-free corpus undiluted by human factors external to its incidence.[48]

Figure 22 contrasts the movement of revelation as expressed in Islam with that found in Christianity. In the one process there is a 'sending down', in the other a 'coming down'. The eternal speech (Word) of God in Islam becomes the book to be recited or spoken on earth. The eternal living person (Word) in Christianity becomes flesh, 'Word incarnate' on earth. To compare the Qur'ân and the Bible is therefore to miss the point. The real comparison is between the Qur'ân and Jesus. The 'Word' is made book in Islam and flesh in Christianity. The nearest equivalent to the Traditions (the ḥadîth literature) is the record enshrined in the four Gospels. The human telling of how God's Word impinges upon mankind is explored in these documents.

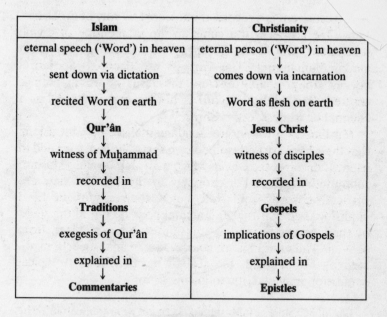

Islam	Christianity
eternal speech ('Word') in heaven	eternal person ('Word') in heaven
↓	↓
sent down via dictation	comes down via incarnation
↓	↓
recited Word on earth	Word as flesh on earth
↓	↓
Qur'ân	**Jesus Christ**
↓	↓
witness of Muḥammad	witness of disciples
↓	↓
recorded in	recorded in
↓	↓
Traditions	**Gospels**
↓	↓
exegesis of Qur'ân	implications of Gospels
↓	↓
explained in	explained in
↓	↓
Commentaries	**Epistles**

Figure 22
Revelation as portrayed in Islam and Christianity

The sense of 'mission' differs also in Islam and Christianity as Figure 23 illustrates. Islam requires uniformity among all would-be Muslims. Indonesians and Turks must learn to read and worship in Arabic if their *islâm* ('submission') is to be meaningful and valid. The movement is strongly centripetal in Islam, calling all to witness in the one tongue and to kneel in the one direction. The incarnation of Christ sets an opposite tone in Christian witness. Just as the eternal Word became the enfleshed Word in Jesus Christ, so the centrifugal movement is to be repeated in Jesus' disciples. It is to be their joy to translate their witness into the languages and cultures of those not yet won to their Lord. The resultant worshipful obedience is gradually to filter out to find expression in all the different languages of human tribes and tongues.

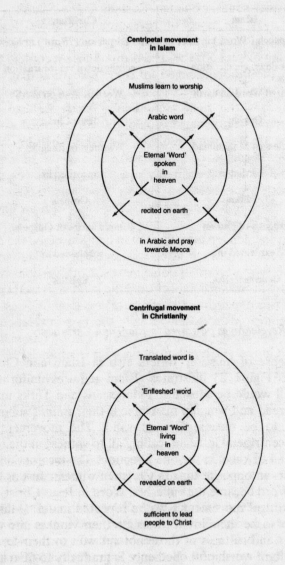

Centripetal movement in Islam

Muslims learn to worship

Arabic word

Eternal 'Word'
spoken
in
heaven

recited on earth

in Arabic and pray
towards Mecca

Centrifugal movement in Christianity

Translated word is

'Enfleshed' word

Eternal 'Word'
living
in
heaven

revealed on earth

sufficient to lead
people to Christ

Figure 23
Sense of 'mission' in Islam and Christianity

The real sting in Salman Rushdie's *The Satanic Verses* comes over the issue of revelation/inspiration. Rushdie embellishes a story, taken from the Traditions, concerning the giving of sura 53, the sura of the Star. According to al-Tabarî, the Prophet longed for some revelation that would soften the call to the Meccans away from their gross polytheism towards the rigid monotheism which he had been preaching. The original version of this sura allowed worship of three of the prime idols of the Quraysh tribe. When Muhammad announced that first version of the sura of the Star, the Meccans reportedly prostrated themselves. Soon Muhammad was taken to task by God who replaced the verses allowing worship of the three idols with an uncompromising statement of monotheism (vv 19–23). The Prophet then understood that Satan had whispered the alternative verses in his ear as he was receiving revelation from Gabriel: they were the satanic verses. Both versions of the sura were proclaimed publicly and the incident is well known by Muslims under the catchphrase 'The Satanic Verses'.

Rushdie's 'joke' is that actually the two 'revelations' of sura 53 are due neither to God's activity nor Satan's. Rushdie has Gibreel (Gabriel) pronounce his (Rushdie's) view on the Muslim's concept of revelation:

> Gibreel, hovering-watching from his highest camera angle, knows one small detail, just one tiny thing that's a bit of a problem here, namely that *it was me both times, baba, me first and second also me*. From my mouth, both the statement and the repudiation, verses and converses, universes and reverses, the whole thing, and we all know how my mouth got worked.[49]

Gibreel gets his mouth worked by 'Mahound' (Muhammad) who forces Gibreel's face open and makes the voice pour out of him 'like sick'. It is Mahound's own voice, own desires, self-revelation. Not only Satan, but also God, are outside Rushdie's view of 'revelation'. It is far from sending down or *tanzîl*; it is self-projection by Muhammad.

There are very few Muslims who entertain a view of revelation or inspiration different from the classical one. Certainly there are few who would agree with Rushdie's restatement and hardly any who would dare express such a restatement in terms as offensive as his. The Muslim norm, with regard to the giving of the Book, is a 'fundamentalist' view.

Thin edge of the wedge?

'Sending down' requires accurate recording and preserving of what has been delivered from heaven to earth. That process was completed with the research and defining done by 'Uthmân. Since the recension absolutised by him, all Qur'âns in Arabic have been the same.[50]

There is hardly any question within Islam of analysing the source and form of the text in the way that the Bible has been treated by the theological schools of source or form criticism. To define the giving of specific verses in terms of Muhammad's psychological or physical needs smells suspiciously like taking the initiative in 'sending down' away from God. What has happened, with that view, to the eternal nature of the heavenly Qur'ân? Where some modern, free-minded Muslims have moved in such a direction they have generally been ostracised by the theologians and jurists of their homelands.[51]

It was gradually accepted, however, that 'sending down' necessitates exegesis and explanation. At first some of the Traditions helped to make clear what the Qur'ânic text meant or in what context verses were given. Gradually commentaries came to be written on the Qur'ân. The science of such Qur'ânic exegesis is known as *tafsîr*. Al-Tabarî, mentioned above in connection with *The Satanic Verses*, was the author of the first commentary. Before his death in AD 923, he had produced a thirty-volume, detailed study of the Qur'ânic text.

It is a small step from exegesis to interpretation. Muslims, reflecting on their own contemporary situations, ask themselves the question: 'What does this text mean for me today, in my age and culture?' Private interpretation moves into the disputed area of pioneering new understandings of the sacred law (*ijtihâd*). Such research and reinterpretation can, of course, be the standard-bearer for completely new elucidations (like the modernists) or renewed expositions (like the Islamists). Both find justification in the process of *ijtihâd* for the overthrow of the theological and/or political status quo.

Taking everything literally

In some respects, therefore, all Muslims operate from a 'fundamentalist' base. Their common stance on 'sending down' (*tanzîl*) betrays a literalist appreciation of their source text which is vastly different from the picture given in the Christian's Scripture. Beyond that common stance, however, there are a variety of approaches to 'being truly Muslim'. The reformist or resurgent Islamist is but one among many.

The reformist Muslim is, undoubtedly, the most literalist. He seeks to place himself within the whole *sharî'a* as revealed. He refuses any but the literalist interpretation and his dependence is upon the Qur'ân and *sunna* as primary sources for law-making (*fiqh*).

A purely 'spiritual' or 'liberal' approach to the Qur'ân in exegesis is unacceptable to the reformist Muslim. We have seen his insistence upon literalism demonstrated in many situations with regard to the duty of *jihâd* or 'holy war'. According to the Islamists, one cannot talk of a 'higher' or spiritual *jihâd*, a kind of war against the world, the flesh and the devil. That is not what the Qur'ân and *sunna* refer to. One has to face up to the reality of armed conflict. Such is the literal meaning of *jihâd* in the source texts.

Similarly, the subjecting of Qur'ânic exegesis to other concerns, such as nationalism or 'Arab socialism', is invalid. Hence Mawdudi's initial reluctance to support the movement within pre-independent India for a separate Muslim homeland. Hence Qutb's distancing from Nasser over the latter's radical land reforms in Egypt.

Muslim mosaic

By and large in the history of Islam, such a literalist approach to the implementation of the whole 'way' or *sharî'a* has remained a minority view. The 'fundamentalist' or reformist option seems only to have found possibility of acceptance, even expression, in a limited number of situations.[52]

No one could reasonably claim that all was hunky-dory in the Muslim empires that controlled most of the Muslim populations of the world before European colonial expansion. Down through the centuries after Muhammad and his Companions, there were various movements of protest against the compromising of Islam. One of the most vociferous objectors of all times was a gentleman from Harran in Mesopotamia. Ahmad Ibn Taimîya (AD 1263–1328) was an outstanding scholar of the Qur'ân and the Traditions. Through pen and word he exposed the shortcomings of his Muslim contemporaries, leaders and people alike. He paid for his outspokenness with prison terms, but his writings have been the inspiration of many Muslim reformist movements. In the late eighteenth and nineteenth centuries, Ibn Taimîya's thoughts strongly influenced the Wahhâbî movement in its successful bid for power and reform in the Islamic heartland of Arabia. In Egypt, this century, the pages of Faraj's *The Neglected Duty* are filled with quotations from Ibn Taimîya.

For the most part, however, Islamic rule in the pre-colonial period stressed *sharî'a* law even though there was often considerable accommodation to local personal or customary rules. For their part, the jurists mostly co-operated with their governments to maintain the status quo.

During the colonial period, there were many Muslim responses to the changed political circumstances. In this book we have concentrated on the reformist or Islamist response. There were, of course, other reactions with their own outstanding proponents, many of whom won the ascendancy in various countries as colonial rule ran its course.

The Young Ottomans in Turkey, for example, sought to make Islam compatible with many Western scientific, economic and political concepts in order to strengthen Turkey against the West. Others tried to adapt Islam to the needs of modern bourgeois societies. Many modernist movements stressed national rather than Islamic identity. Aḥmad Kasravi sought this ethnic identity in Iran, while Arab nationalism was strong among the Arab countries with large non-Muslim minorities.

In the post-colonial era, there has emerged a common pattern of state control over religion. This was markedly the case in Atatürk's Turkey and Riza Shah's Iran. It has also been the situation in many nations where secular nationalism has become the underlying political philosophy. In those nations one of the processes going on at present is a gradual inclusion of more *sharīʿa* law, at least for Muslims, as part of the price for maintaining the political status quo in a world where resurgent Islam seems to have a growing voice.[53]

The contemporary reformist movements in Islam appear to have capitalised on the 'failures' of secular nationalism. It is significant that reformist Islam is not strong in states which are still largely traditional and which have avoided a major Western cultural impact. The Yemen Arab Republic (united with the Yemen People's Democratic Republic in 1990 to form the Republic of Yemen) and Saudi Arabia would be two cases in point. By contrast, those countries which have known a high degree of secularisation and the importation of

Western cultural values seem to be more fertile ground for recruitment to the reformist perspective today. Iran, Egypt, Tunisia, Algeria, Nigeria and Malaysia all boast considerably virile movements for ideological change among their Muslim populations.

Turkey and Pakistan are different again, though in both there exist recent Islamising movements which have brought considerable pressure to bear upon the society in general (Turkey) or upon a government in particular (Pakistan). Yet Turkey remains the most secularised, Western-oriented Muslim country in terms of its institutionalised life, while Pakistan's populations found life after Zia in a woman premier, Benazir Bhutto.

Iran seems to be the only country widely recognised as comprising an 'Islamic government' in the mould of the reformist Muslims. Does such recognition, however, communicate admiration for the implementation of the government of God itself or for the guts of a state and a statesman that have successfully stood up to the West?

Simply reactionary?

It would be wrong to dismiss the various twentieth-century reformist movements as simply a desire to return to the good old days, a longing for the past, a craving for medieval Islam. They are, rather, part of the mix of responses and counter-responses to rapidly changing conditions in Muslim countries around the globe.

In the fight for independence from colonial rule, a variety of mutually exclusive Muslim views became temporary bedfellows. In the sorting out of post-colonial societies, the reformists have until recently mostly comprised a protest movement, a thorn in the side of governments which are culturally, economically and politically dependent upon the West.

Who can predict the kind of alignment of circumstances in

any one nation which will promote a population's espousal of the Islamists' ideological view? Who can predict the rise of a 'strong Khomeini versus a cancer-stricken Shah' in countries other than Iran? Who can tell whether Muslim grievances with Western nations or their indigenous protégés will become serious enough for masses of Muslims to demand resurgent Islam or nothing?

CHAPTER TWENTY

RULED OUT?

On a bicycle built for one

WORLDVIEWS TEND TO BE SELF-AFFIRMING and the worldview of the Muslim reformist is no exception. It all makes sense if seen from that particular viewpoint. The Muslim reformist, moreover, believes his worldview to be God's perspective and so absolutely right. It is a question of convincing the rest of the world of the 'truth'.

Interrelated themes bubble to the surface when we consider how contemporary Muslim reformists relate to the larger communities in which they are set. Can the Islamist come to terms with living as one variety of voice in a pluralistic society? How does resurgent Islam relate to minority other-faith groups within the country where its voice is in the ascendancy? What attitude does the reformist Muslim hold towards those from his own faith community who express a desire to change their religious allegiance? How comfortably does the Islamist interact with the majority culture when his own position is that of a minority voice?

Live and let live?

Most nations of our world are pluralist in terms of the make-up of their populace. In Islamic countries, for example, the varieties include ethnic groups, Sunnî or Shî'a sects, adherents of four major schools of law, members of mystical (Sûfî) orders, those who mix Islam with Marxism, socialism or capitalism, people with different linguistic identities, those whose worldview is predominantly that of popular Islam, and, of course, the Islamists. This is quite apart from varieties of social class, economic clout, educational background, political power holdings, and so on.

The harsh reality is that reformist visionaries have no patience with any but their own interpretation of how Muslims should be organised politically. They see their own perspective as the only valid perspective. From visionary to visionary there may be considerable difference of detail but there is a surprising amount of cross-fertilisation. We have noted the strong influence of Mawdudi's ideas on Qutb. The works of some of the Shî'a scholars such as Shariati, Khomeini and Ayatollah Muhammad Bâqir al-Ṣadr have been published by the Sunnî-founded Islamic Organisation in Pakistan and Muslim Brotherhood in Arab countries. Equally, the writings of Mawdudi, Banna, Qutb and others have been published by the Shî'a communities of Qum.

We need to bear in mind that the reformist visionary is not a reactionary in the sense of simply demanding a return to the past while turning his back on the modern world. The mindset is different from, say, the Amish of North America. The reformist Muslim distinguishes between development and modernisation on the one hand and Westernisation and secularisation on the other. His goal is to draw on the resources of the contemporary world as well as on the original sources of Islam so that Muslims' lives are positively modernised. That goal has, however, to be achieved without compromising basic Islamic principles and values.

Muslims of the twentieth century believe that God has

given them a huge practical resource in oil. With oil comes money and power, massive clout in a world that is economically and politically increasingly bound together. The visionaries' aim is to use those resources to better the Muslim community (the *umma*), to advance the cause of Islam and to bring mankind to live in the kind of society that God intends. Machinery and medical expertise, space conquest and satellite TV, well-ordered infrastructures and computer-guided economies are fine so long as their use is not the result of some kind of blind aping of the West.

The reformist Muslim's argument is, therefore, with everyone. It is an ideological battle. The compromised Islam of post-colonial secular Muslim states is unacceptable. The Marxist atheism and the capitalist 'Christian' alternatives of the wealthy Northern countries are anathema. All that falls short of the rule of God is to be castigated and replaced.

The pluralist sentiment in which mankind learns to live and let live is obviously foreign to an ideology which says that only one worldview is universally valid. It is especially alien to an ideology which allows for force to convince those who doubt. Expressions of this more harsh sentiment come to the surface when the mindset of the Islamic reformists wins supremacy.

In Pakistan under Zia the issue of female emancipation became a focal point of attempted domination by the hard-line ideologists and of women's striving to retain the 'freedoms' which they felt had been validly won in a Muslim secular society. In post-revolution Iran the cruel searching out and elimination of Bahais has demonstrated a spirit which will force aside alternative views rather than re-educate or coexist with their adherents.

Aliens for ever?

The treatment of aliens or strangers is an acid test of the spirit of a majority culture. From ancient times until today most societies seem to fall far short of what the Bible declares is God's intention. The Muslim reformists' stance is no exception.

Minorities are, of course, accepted within an Islamic state, but only as second-class citizens (*dhimmîs*). We noted earlier what Mawdudi felt this would entail.[54] To some extent Mawdudi has had his way. Christians and Hindus in Pakistan under Zia have discovered what it feels like to be reidentified as different kinds of people from the majority culture, a difference enshrined in revised voting patterns at elections. The setting up of separate electorates for religious minorities means that minorities can only vote for their own candidates (of whom there is a fixed number) in national, provincial and local elections. Those candidates naturally represent much larger geographical areas and are consequently that much further removed from the realities of life of the people they are supposed to represent.

In Egypt, a lot of the focus of the Muslim reformists in their attempts to wrest control of the country has centred in acts of aggression against Christians. During 1990, for example, major rioting occurred in several southern Egyptian cities and their surrounding villages. One riot arose out of a rumour that Christians had compromised the honour of two Muslim girls who were the daughters of the local judge in a certain town. As a result of the rumour, crowds attacked and burned several churches and many properties owned by Christians. In the coastal city of Alexandria, a Coptic priest and his wife and friends were machine-gunned to death by militant Muslims.

In the Islamic Republic of Iran, persecution of Christians has focused strongly on the Anglican Church. A year after the revolution, Aristo Sayeh, a vicar in Shiraz, was found with his throat slit. Attempts were made on the life of the bishop, Hasan Deqhani-Tafti, and the bishop's son was assassinated on a Tehran street. Armenian and Assyrian Christians have also been singled out for liquidation.

Christians, and others, in Indonesia face the continual manoeuvring of members of the Muslim majority to transform the society, currently based on the 'Five Principles' (*pancasila*), into an Islamic state.

The ideology of the Muslim reformists is quite clear about the position of minority peoples. In their view they are human beings of value and dignity, honour and even faith ('People of the Book'), but they are not Muslims, not truly submitted to God. The role they are allowed to have in society is therefore carefully curtailed and controlled.

It is one of the marks of movement in many Muslim nations today that Islamic law (the *sharî'a*) is being increasingly applied. In some cases, such as Iran or Pakistan, this is being done as part of the willed programme of the people in power. In other cases, such as Egypt and Sudan, regimes appear to be conceding some tightening of Islamic law as the price of avoiding more stringent demands. The processes, willed or conceded, augur ill for those minority peoples within the countries concerned. The prognosis for their continued health and 'freedom', in societies which are being increasingly wooed to a more reformist worldview, is bleak.

Black sheep?

Even more bleak is the situation of those who are Muslim by birth and upbringing, yet who choose as adults to change their religious allegiance. Reformist Islam is sure about its dealing with 'apostates', those who turn their backs on Islam. They are not to be tolerated.

As far as the Qur'ân is concerned there is punishment for apostasy, but the clearest consideration of the subject, in sura 3, suggests that such punishment takes effect after this life:

If anyone desires
A religion other than
Islam (submission to God),
Never will it be accepted
Of him; and in the Hereafter
He will be in the ranks
Of those who have lost
(All spiritual good) (sura 3:85).

Sometimes, however, an appeal is made to a different verse of the Qur'ân concerning the possibility of punishment in this life for the sin of apostasy:

The punishment of those
Who wage war against God
And His Apostle, and strive
With might and main
For mischief through the land
Is: execution, or crucifixion,
Or the cutting off of hands
And feet from opposite sides,
Or exile from the land:
That is their disgrace
In this world, and
A heavy punishment is theirs
In the Hereafter (sura 5:36).

Al-Bukhârî, compiler of one of the two major lists of Traditions (hadîth) recognised by Sunnî Muslims, quotes this verse of the Qur'ân at the beginning of his section dealing with apostasy. He goes on to record Traditions in which the Prophet punished apostasy with death.[55]

Certainly, on the basis of the treatment of the subject in the Traditions, jurists have concluded that apostasy from Islam is punishable by death in certain cases. They disagree concerning the details of which cases qualify for death and which don't.

Mawdudi was in no doubt that in an Islamic state there

could be no room for Muslims to change their faith. His view is the norm for reformist visionaries, though there are shades of opinion as to whether the agent of conversion should also be punished, and if so, how severely.

Egypt has consistently bowed to this reformist interpretation of 'freedom of religion' in her handling of Muslims who profess faith in Christ. Adverts in the national dailies in the 1980s guaranteed that the Ministry of Justice in Cairo would facilitate the conversion of anyone from 'anything' to Islam in under one hour. There were no facilities for movement in the opposite direction. The law about such movement in the other direction is grey. The practice is quite clear and many Christians from Muslim backgrounds have spent time in prison for their faith in the past two decades, with at least one dying there.

In Iran, where a significant minority group of Christians from a Muslim background has developed since 1979, the Islamic government has deliberately sought to repress it. One church leader from this group has been in prison for over five years with no news of his fate. Another pastor in the Assemblies of God, himself from a Muslim background, was tortured and executed because of his faith in December 1990.

Such a dealing with 'apostasy' hardly sits comfortably with a commitment to the upholding of universal human rights. Most Muslim countries are signatories to the United Nations Declaration of Human Rights (1948). Yet, can a Muslim really exercise his right to change his faith?

Our study in worldview should help us answer this question. The major problem revolves around the meaning 'faith' has in a people's outlook on life. In Western terms, to change faith allegiance is a reasonable option given that 'faith allegiance' is not ultimate or foundational in a secularist view of the world.

'Faith' means far more in a Muslim reformist's conception of what life is all about. The reformist's abhorrence of apostasy tends naturally to infiltrate a society which sees allegiance to Islam as more than just a personal faith-option. To change 'faith' means to turn one's back on family, clan, nation and the only valid way of living. Consequently, Muslims who change allegiance often do so secretly, or they leave their community (often their country) or they are punished in one form or another up to the ultimate sentence.

How should we then live?

The worldview of the Islamist is not only distant from that of Western, secular, liberal man on this point. It also moves a long way from the cultural mandate of the Bible, where a plurality of societies find validity in God's eyes and need to discover ways of accommodating one another in their own eyes. In a world of marred social beings, the wonderful possibility is suggested in the Old Testament that individuals and nations should answer to God for their 'sins' rather than to fellow human beings. The Lord will use a Babylonian emperor to exact his punishment on Judah's apostasy, but the emperor himself is not the judge, merely a servant awaiting his Master's whistle. The servant will be punished where he takes the law into his own hands (Isaiah 13–14).

The ethnic puritanism of Ezra and Nehemiah comes closest in the Old Testament to a spirit of exclusivism. For the most part, the Hebrew Scriptures are intensely inclusivist in terms of God's blessing being extended to all the nations of the earth. The early covenants reach to all peoples and the Lord chooses Abraham/Israel deliberately so that all the nations of the earth might be blessed (Genesis 12:3). For her part, little Israel is humbly to accept God's love for the Queen of Sheba (1 Kings 10) or the cattle of Nineveh (Jonah 4:11) or 'anointed' Cyrus (Isaiah 45:1). She is at the same time to keep herself pure by refusing the nations' idolatrous faith-allegiances and sticking to the Lord with all her heart. The tension of remaining pure towards the Lord and open towards the nations was difficult to handle. Solomon erred in one direction, Jonah in another. Neither diplomatic idolatry nor religious ethnocentrism were God's calling to Israel. He chose her to cherish and obey her Lord and to serve the nations.

'Serving the nations' won't necessarily be a pleasant business. Jesus' disciples are specifically commanded to witness on his behalf to all mankind. The preciousness of martyrdom through the New Testament's continuing saga of mission suggests that such declaring for Christ will always be a challenge to whatever worldview is being confronted. Religious leaders connive at a stoning (Acts 7:57), a politician swings the sword to deplete the disciples' number (Acts 12:2) and idol-makers throw apostles out of town (Acts 19). To be known as belonging to the community of the Christian faithful has in many societies in many centuries required faithfulness unto death. Human worldviews do not readily accommodate the Christ.

At the same time, certain New Testament passages suggest that God is very concerned about faithfulness and integrity in his people. A 'spiritual' dynamic, reminding one of the law of apostasy in Islam, appears to operate for those who walk the Christian 'Way' (Acts 9:2) and then turn their backs on Christ. It seems that Ananias and Sapphira had but told a pretty small fib about their dealings on the property market. The Lord took it very personally. Little wonder that 'great fear' seized the whole church and those who heard about the incident. Who could have predicted that the nascent Christian community would be so severely disciplined (Acts 5:1–11)? Weren't Christians dead and buried in Corinth also because they had reneged on their commitment to the 'body of Christ' (1 Corinthians 11:30)?

Both Old Testament and New address the issue of faithfulness to God. Both reserve the right of judgement to the Lord himself. Human agents of such judgement are only servants, not masters. They are themselves subject to evaluation. Apostasy is deadly serious, but it is the Lord who looks on the human heart and says, 'Thus far and no further.' Human attempts to abrogate such a right to themselves (as with Jonah outside Nineveh or with Jesus' disciples outside a hostile Samaritan village) are absolutely rejected.

The history of the church in both West and East, and probably the angry feelings within Christians' hearts towards one another today, bespeak an attitude similar to that manifested by Islamists over the matter of apostasy. Christians also, with hand or heart, condemn to death those viewed as heretics, schismatics, unfaithful or simply different. Anger, in Jesus' eyes, is usually equivalent to murder (Matthew 5:21). We all easily find verses of Scripture to justify our own particular positions and to condemn the rest. Our attitudes differ little from those of the 'fundamentalists'.

In biblical terms, apostasy is God's problem and has to be handled in his way. By the scriptural standard we all fall far short.

The shoe on the other foot

One of the long-term effects of imperialism and the rebuilding of Western economies after World War II has been the establishment in Europe of significant communities of Muslims. Those communities have tended to reflect the forms that Islam has taken in their countries of origin. Where the Islamic reformists have had significant influence on affairs in those countries, they have also extended such influence into the minority groups in Europe.

There has been an increasingly vocal call by Muslims in Europe for the accommodation in Western society of some of the outworkings of their worldview. The areas that they are most concerned about include the details of their children's education, the importance of Friday prayers, and the provision of ritually slaughtered meat. In many ways Muslims feel marginalised by the majority culture in societies built upon secular, democratic foundations. They certainly feel misunderstood as is evident from the uproar over Salman Rushdie in the United Kingdom. From their perspective, every forward step towards a situation in which they consider they are practically able to function as Muslims has come about only by painfully slow negotiation.

Figure 24 enumerates some of the issues currently being raised by British Muslims in the area of 'religious education'. In their view, all aspects of education, including the form in which it is offered, have to come to the bar of *sharî'a* standards. All education is, in that primary sense, 'religious'.

Area of Concern	Muslim Demands
Curriculum	Teaching of Islam by competent authorities Exemption from sex education Non-mixed physical education and swimming classes Teaching of mother tongue
Social customs	Modest clothing for girls as part of uniform Availability of lawfully killed (*halâl*) food Holidays for the main Muslim celebrations
Staffing	Employment of more Muslim staff (eg, there are fewer than 15 Muslim teachers out of 11,000 in the Birmingham Local Education Authority)
Piety	Appropriate morning assemblies

Figure 24
Muslims and 'religious education' in the United Kingdom

From the host cultures' perspective, it seems so unfair that mosques are being built all over the Western world while it is still impossible to build churches in Saudi Arabia, notwithstanding the fact that a substantial minority of Christians are residing there, contributing to the country's growth. For some Christians within the host nations of the West, every church converted into a mosque or every school authority giving in to Muslim parents' demands concerning codes of dress is a defeat before Satan's onslaught.

The issues are many and complex. The picture broadens to embrace a situation like that in the Philippines where the Muslim minority feels it has no alternative to armed insurrection in order to obtain a 'fair deal' in a country predominantly Roman Catholic and dominated by the 'Christian' United States of America.

Is there hope for a meeting of minds, a mutual recognition of each community's differences, yet a willingness to be counted together as citizens, even (in a Britain with a vestige of national Christian commitment) co-religionists?

The secularist worldview says that the living together of incompatibles is a possibility if only 'religion' is interpreted as private piety. The West can allow Muslims their mosques; the Muslim world should allow Christians their churches. A British Muslim could become a Member of Parliament, even Prime Minister; Muslim societies should allow the possibility for a non-Muslim to hold significant office.

The Islamic reformist worldview says that you cannot hive off 'religion' from the rest of life. You have to learn to be faithful to God in all or not at all. Within the domain of true Islamic rule (*dâr al-Islâm*), the issues have been sorted out and hopefully approximate to God's will. The goal is to bring the rest of mankind to such submission. Where reformist Muslims live as minority communities in secular societies, they have to act as thorns in the flesh constantly pushing for closer approximation to what should pertain under God's government. Where non-Muslims live as minority communities in Muslim societies, they are to be treated as valid human beings and may of course live as members of the wider community without being forced to convert to Islam; but they live as *dhimmîs*, as second-class citizens. There is no question of tit-for-tat: a church in the centre of Riyadh for a mosque in Regent's Park.

The Islamic 'system' is God-sanctioned, while the secular 'system' is human-born. Western secularist and Islamic reformist are worldviews apart.

CHAPTER TWENTY-ONE

SLAUGHTERERS' APPRENTICE

Y OUNG ALI ADJUSTED THE MASK over his nose and mouth. He nodded in understanding to his older brother, Talal. The battered van turned off the smooth boulevard and crashed over the rough sidestreets towards the hotel district.

A battle lull allowed both sides to retrieve their fallen martyrs. Makeshift ambulances scurried from East and West of the city to the latest point of armed argument. Death's gains were briefly celebrated as 'our heroes' in motorised tours of Christian or Muslim Beirut before the bosses redistributed the depleted workforces.

Talal had briefed his brother as he drove the old meat van to the starting point for the Muslim convoy.

'If anyone asks, say you are fifteen, Ali. No one wants responsibility for a twelve-year-old in this business.'

Talal had only agreed to taking Ali along with him because at the short notice given he couldn't rouse Mansour. The word had been passed quickly to bring the 'martyr wagons' to the beginning of the airport road. There, they should wait for instructions to go in and retrieve the dead and dying. Mansour had disappeared into thin air that morning and Ali pestered Talal to let him go in his place.

'When we go into the building, little brother, you take

205

short, shallow breaths. Like this.' Talal demonstrated, panting at the wheel.

Ali grinned and began to giggle.

'Not funny, young one! Put on that mask and get used to the feel of it. Now pant!'

Ali fumbled with the strings of the mask. Having secured it after a fashion over nose and mouth, he settled down to learning the tricks of a meat trade his butcher father had never dreamed about.

'It will be dark inside the hotel. Stick close to me. Keep moving till I say "This brother!" or "That brother!" Work fast, pant fast and keep within hearing of my voice. We may not have long.'

Talal acknowledged the horns of other vehicles making for the assembly point: sharp pointed stabs of sound, nods of the head as the dealers in death congregated like tamed vultures ready to collect their pickings.

'Lay the blanket completely over the body. Take breaths through your mouth. Then quickly turn the body over onto the blanket and draw the rest of the cloth over him. Turn away and breathe and don't look! You will work with Taki's cousin. He is strong. You handle the feet.'

'I am strong, big brother. Look!' Ali's voice exploded through the linen mask as he seized Talal's wrist, pulling with all his might.

'Do you want to add us to those going in the back? Leave go!' shouted Talal as he fought to compensate for the sudden downward tug on the steering wheel.

'Trust me, Ali,' he muttered as he gained control of the vehicle and himself. 'It is not physical strength you lack. In there, it is more than physical strength that is needed. So, this first time, you take the feet, okay?'

Ali conceded and sank back in the seat aware that his brother was talking seriously about something he knew nothing of, as yet.

'When all the bodies on that floor are ready we bring them

down to the vans. One floor at a time. We don't leave till all the vans are full. When we go, we go fast! At least, to the boulevard!'

The orientation had been abandoned as the brothers joined the group swelling at the end of the airport road, waiting for the order to go in.

Now the trail of battered hearses, slogan-daubed and postered, sped quietly towards the hotel district. They would be a lot more noisy on their way back. Horns blaring, guns firing, Beirut would know that Islamic martyrs were being royally escorted to their final resting place.

The van lurched in the sidestreet as a front wheel hit a pothole. Probably a grenade-made crater from the battle just ended. Talal and Ali rode the movement as they kept their eyes above the road, searching out the militia soldier who would guide them to their building.

Ali swallowed hard, frightened and thrilled at his twelve-year-old part in this incredible *jihâd*.

CHAPTER TWENTY-TWO

THE FINAL WORD

Beyond sloganeering

PRESIDENT SADAT OF EGYPT HAD A 'SLOGAN WAR' with the Muslim Brothers in the 1970s. Sadat shouted: *'Lâ siyâsa fî'l-dîn wa lâ dîn fî'l-siyâsa'* ('no politics in religion and no religion in politics'). The Brothers screamed back: *'Al-islâm dîn wa dawla'* ('Islam is both a religion and a state').

Sadat and the reformist Muslims were light-years apart in their approaches, despite the appeal by both to Islamic heritage and to their own piety. Sadat fell short, in the Islamists' view, because 'Islam' was not *the* central principle but just one component in the state's ideology. The Islamists erred, in the President's view, because their 'Islam' was immature and bigoted, unsuitable for an Egypt which needed to find its way in the pluralist, economically complex world of the twentieth century. The war of worldview was waged and worsened by prison terms and sudden assassination.

The chapters of this book have traced in detail something of the Islamists' critique of the Muslim status quo in different countries and through various decades of this century. That critique has been founded upon a commitment to the original sources of Islam in the Qur'ân and prophetic example (*sunna*). It has evolved within a series of movements which have been ideological and universalist in their appeal, far from nationalistic or sectarian. In increasingly radical ways, the Islamists have declared the muddied mixture of post-colonial Muslim states unattractive and unfaithful.

By implication, therefore, and often quite explicitly stated, the upheavals of Islamic resurgence also represent a critique of Western culture. For it was Western culture which impinged so heavily on Muslim peoples during colonial rule and it is Western culture which remains strongly influential in many Muslim countries since independence. It is Western culture and civilisation which brings to bear upon Muslim populations a totally different view of the world.

At foundation, the Western worldview is infused with the spirit of secular humanism. The theocentric worldview of Islam quickly exposes that spirit: to the reformist Muslim it is obvious that the Westerner is a non-believing materialist. One proponent of resurgent Islam has expressed the common view in simple, almost wistful words:

> ...I would like to invite my western colleagues to understand that Muslim criticism of Western civilization is not primarily an exercise in political confrontation. The real competition would be at the level of two cultures and civilizations, one based upon Islamic values and the other on the values of materialism and nationalism. Had western culture been based on Christianity, on morality, on faith, the language and *modus operandi* of the contact and conflict would have been different. But that is not the case. The choice is between the Divine Principle and a secular materialist culture.[56]

Christianity, morality and faith?

Horror of hostage-taking, plane-hijacking and mass demonstration against foreign influence in Middle Eastern nations has perhaps fooled Westerners into thinking that the 'problems' of civilisation are all in the Muslim camp. It's the Islamists who are crude, inhumane, irrational. Their world is the world of bigotry, fanaticism and 'spiritual darkness'.

Our study of the complex interaction of East and West in producing the current climate for Muslim 'fundamentalist' overdrive suggests that 'the West' does have something to do with the tensions between Muslim and Westerner in today's world. It takes two to make an argument. To listen just a little to the Islamists' view of the world helps us appreciate that some of our contemporaries choose to see things in a way radically different from our own. Might there not be some good reasons for their so doing?

The collision of strongly differentiated worldviews can help us look afresh at ourselves as well as looking at the others. The discovery of what the Islamists value as important can assist us in recognising the major themes of our own outlook on life. Resurgent Islam's critique of the Western worldview should provoke us to stop and reflect.

Is it not true that humanism is enthroned in the institutions of our country? We pay lip-service to a hangover from the days when the sovereign could call the nation to prayer and fasting. We have a peculiar institutionalisation of the Church of England as a 'state religion'. The reality is, however, that our country works by the philosophy that rationalism, rather than God, will guide, protect and prosper us. The lords spiritual may have a voice in the Upper House, but it is the common voice of rational thought in the Lower House which constitutes the motor force of our law-making.

Is it not true that we live in a secularised society? The way to handle all our ethnic, cultural and religious differences is to bury them before the altar of secularisation. The assumptions which govern the worlds of politics, economics, education and culture urge us along the road of secularisation.

What works economically to increase our share in the international market is the motive governing our industry and commerce. We do not primarily consider what the

Creator intends by making us tenants of *his* good earth. Who in 'the City' sees that frenzied financial world as God's? We do not formulate national budgets with a view to giving to those poorer than ourselves. Rationalisation, industrialisation and urbanisation have become marks of a society moving away from a vision of people as made in the image of God, worthy of work and with integral dignity. Instead people are transformed into statistics, union-fodder, numbers of unemployed, 'natural wastage', obstinates who refuse to 'get on their bikes' and go where 'the market' dictates.

In our Western world, Christianity is one among many religious possibilities, all of which are permitted options. Permitted, that is, so long as they remain in the private domain. Tolerated, so long as no Member of Parliament stands up in the House of Commons to embarrass people with statements like 'The Bible says....' Allowed, so long as no school teacher claims that the biblical 'myth' is far more valid than the secularisation 'myth'.

We are sixth-generation children of the Enlightenment and it is becoming increasingly plain in our culture that 'secularisation' is not the benign or neutral god our fathers believed it to be. Within our British model of national life, it is clear that 'secularised society' is but a posh name for 'pagan society'. Our culture has its gods. What others from outside (like reformist Muslims) have long seen clearly, we from inside are beginning to uncover.

'Freedom of the individual' transposes so easily into 'breakdown of the family'. We don't marry up to four wives like those Muslims, oh no, but we do engage in sequential polygamy! We marry, divorce and remarry almost at will. Most young people come to marriage today already experienced in sexual relationships (okay so long as it is 'safe') and we think we have stable 'civilisation' to pass on to the 'developing' nations. There is no religious favouritism in our secular society, except that our TV programmes, school textbooks and public arts are loaded with references to the occult. We are not barbarians, but our national accounts only balance because we produce weapons of war with which others can destroy themselves at their own expense.

The joke is on us. Our 'myth' of what civilised society constitutes is exploding. How come New Age concepts make such strong religious inroads in a supposedly secular society? How come we witness so much mindless violence in our cities? How come we so easily destroy the environment by limitless consumerism? How come the majority of our children will not know what it means to grow up with one set of 'mummy and daddy'?

I think that we have to admit that the Islamist's diagnosis-at-a-distance of the Western worldview is largely accurate. It is not completely exact for there are aspects of our outlook on life that are deeply informed by a Christian ethic. That ethic and the values it endorses have sourced many of the institutionalised peculiarities of our British way of life. The Church of England is one prime example; the controversial 'blasphemy laws' another. 'Christendom' has its hangovers in contemporary British expectations at times of rite of passage such as birth (followed by baptism), marriage (in church) and death (with a Christian service). The teachings of Christ lie vaguely behind much of the sensitivity to created life enshrined in the 'human rights' approach to social dynamics. Nevertheless, there is a lot of perceptiveness in the Islamists' general reading of the contemporary Western worldview.

'Modern' Christians at what price?

The Islamist's holistic worldview especially forces a sober assessment upon those of us who consider ourselves people of faith. The Islamist has a worldview of *tawḥîd* ('oneness' or coherence in God). What do we have? As Christians, is it not true that we have mostly agreed in the secularisation story?

It seems to me that we have, by and large, co-operated in the enthronement of a secular humanist view of the world as the 'modern' face of Western man.

In our zeal for being honest to God and to one another we have 'demythologised' the Bible and brought it up to date. Contemporary science says that miracles are impossible, so we have taken the miracles out of the biblical history and blamed them on those immature, credulous souls of former ages. The resultant bare 'facts' have caused modern Christians a crisis of faith worse than their former crisis of relevancy, for now the essentials of the Gospels (the resurrection, the virgin birth, the 'signs' of Jesus) have gone. On what is modern Christian 'faith' to be based?

Many reading this book cry 'Not me!' Evangelicals, and others, have commendably stood by the biblical text and dared to believe that it properly records unbelievable events which did occur. Their understanding is that modern man refuses to follow the evidence to its proper conclusion: his need of forgiveness, rescuing and remaking. A subtler co-operation with the secular humanist view of the world occurs in this stand against the demythologisers. In order to survive as believers in a non-believing world, the faithful retreat into private faith. The spheres of the arts, politics, medicine, education and the 'social gospel' are carefully avoided for fear of contamination. The crisis of faith for modern man is won but at the expense of a crisis of relevancy in the modern world. Such Christians have largely opted out of declaring the Bible's content to be public truth, universally valid. Instead we have submitted to the secularist proposition that 'faith in the Word of God' is a private matter, all right to adhere to individually, but not for the world at large. We have hived off Sunday and a whole sub-culture of what goes on inside our church walls. We now flounder as we seek to bring some of the assumptions of our faith to bear upon life in the office, life in school, life in the factory, life in the bank, life at home.

In sad and subtle ways, the secular humanism of our Western societies has made huge inroads into the attitudes we hold towards belief in God. Only in recent decades have Western Christians made significant steps forward in terms of moving from private to public expressions of faith, from individual to communal norms for living out a life of discipleship.

Resurgent Islam and Christ

It is not necessarily true, however, that reformist Islam would have had a different history had it encountered a Western culture based on 'Christianity, morality and faith'. Reformist Muslims have come across some individual representatives of Western culture who are vibrant Christians with strong morals and who exercise faith. Western culture has been considerably informed by a Christian ethic, and altruism has marked the soul of many a 'colonialist'.

There is something about the essence of Christianity itself which is always objectionable to faithful Muslims. That essential kernel of the Christian gospel is incapable of being accommodated by Islam. Part of the worldview of (reformist) Islam revolves around a particular view of God as never to be obstructed by mere man. God, in Islam, is God to whom submission is due, not God to be manipulated or with whom one might argue. You cannot change his mind, you cannot cause him to suffer. If tiny man could block God's purposes, to what meaninglessness has *tawḥîd* been diluted?

Muhammad was a prophet of God and as such learned in Medina to model his caliphate or leadership on a philosophy of 'God's side is always successful'. Endemic in the common Muslim interpretation of the Qur'ânic record of Jesus is the conviction that God could not possibly have allowed such a prophet of his to have failed. God would never have allowed the Jews to grab and kill his man. The truth must have been that God took the visage of Jesus and imposed it upon another human being at the crucial moment. Thus Jesus was raised to heaven and someone else (maybe Judas) was crucified in his stead. No Jew could cross God.

Imam Khomeini reflects this Islamic impatience with Jesus. When he is illustrating how Islam is a religion in which divine commands have a political dimension, he questions the biblical record concerning Jesus on politics:

> I do not believe that Jesus held the views on this question of religion and politics that are now attributed to him. Could Jesus ever have taught people to accept oppression? All the prophets, including Jesus, were sent to root out injustice, but later, institutions arose that distorted the nature of religion.[57]

On several occasions Imam Khomeini ridicules the possibility of a 'weak' Jesus. The idea of a prophet who ultimately yields the initiative to his enemies is unthinkable:

> This idea of turning the other cheek has been wrongly attributed to Jesus (peace be upon him); it is those barbaric imperialists that have attributed it to him. Jesus was a prophet, and no prophet can be so illogical.[58]

Khomeini's point is valid insofar as he is objecting to the passive acceptance of institutionalised evil. It is no good arguing that Jesus said, 'Turn the other cheek,' if that appeal is merely an excuse for not challenging the tyranny of wicked rulers. The Imam is, however, objecting to far more than that. A prophet of God has to be successful because God's reputation is at stake. Jesus could never be slapped and purposely allow himself to be slapped again. Jesus is God's man. God's sovereignty has to be defended, by demonstration, on earth.

Islam cannot cope with a 'suffering' Messiah, a 'failed'

mission, a rejection of God's messenger. The tenor of Islam and the conviction of the Islamists is that God wills his divine Word to become reality. Success and power, even coercion, belong to God and to those who fight in God's way. Suffering servant? Never! In the words of Bishop Newbigin: 'The Prophet rode into Mecca to conquer; Jesus rode into Jerusalem to die. The crux lies there.'[59]

Only the Islamists?

It is not only Muslims who display a 'fundamentalist' face in the late twentieth century. The strong rejectionism of the Zionist expression of Judaism carries similar credentials. The fear of destruction (or merely absorption) by the neighbouring Arab communities makes pluralist living in Israel/Palestine an elusive affair. Like reformist Islam, the religious dimension of Zionism is highly politicised, colouring the internal debates and outward expressions of the State of Israel.[60]

Sikhism and Hinduism both know their strains of single-minded 'worldviewedness'. Commitment to such radical expressions of religious allegiance threatens the democratic process in India in the late twentieth century in a way that augurs ill for internal communal stability in that land.

Indeed, one wonders whether the urgent need for some kind of pluralist equilibrium in our modern world serves only to inflame the exclusivisms. Is it the necessity of relating to one another which highlights the inbred ethnocentredness of us all? We didn't know we couldn't get on together until it became plain that we had to!

'Fundamentalism' has its Christian face also. The 'slaughterers' apprentice' of the previous chapter could equally have been a young Christian lad from East Beirut. Lebanon and Northern Ireland perhaps mark the most tragic contemporary expressions of 'militant' Christianity. Less violent, but equally sad, is the rigidity of heart found in exclusivist Orthodoxy,

Catholicism, Protestantism and evangelicalism. Although expressed differently, such Christian 'fundamentalism' is parallel to Islamism in its attempts at cornering 'God'. Such cornering is exemplified by the manipulation of vast Christian subcultures (especially in the United States) by 'fundamentalist' media personalities.

Conservative evangelicalism can sadly become unhealthily 'fundamentalist' in its self-confidence and control of 'truth'. What is so good in conservative evangelicalism (reliance on the Scriptures, insistence upon justification by faith in Christ, assurance of salvation, and so on) can easily become the 'property' of the culturally-limited creature. God is then allowed to work only in the propositionally permitted ways that we set up. We lose sight of the scriptural insistence that 'truth' is primarily personal and relational.

One commentator describes the essence of 'fundamentalism' as the 'cultural annexation of God'.[61] Examples of attempts to annex God to a particular way of looking at life abound in the Bible.

In the Old Testament, for example, Job's 'comforters' exhibit this tendency. After a week of silence and sympathy, they move on to the attack. Their equation is simple: sickness is a result of sin; Job is sick; Job must have sinned. When Job asserts his innocence, they revel in the poor fellow's protests, for in making them, Job is proving their point. How dare Job say that his situation is God's fault? They pull out all the stops to defend God and in doing so squeeze the Lord into their mould for him. The larger picture of the Book of Job is that God is well able to defend himself against Satan, against the 'comforters', against Job. The equation is not simple. The context is bigger than the 'comforters' ever dreamed, more awesome than Job could know, more gracious than Satan imagined. God is God.

Other attempts at cultural annexation in the New Testament are exposed as at variance with Jesus' way. At one point, Jesus' highly motivated disciples see a man driving out demons in his name. The adrenalin rises quickly! Someone is presenting the good news of Jesus without reference to themselves. This person is not 'official'; his doctrines haven't been vetted nor his practices approved! The 'outsider' should be stopped. 'We told him to stop, because he was not one of us,' the disciples report to their Master. Interestingly, Jesus' final word in this matter is very fuzzy. He doesn't say, 'Well he has this minimum content, so we'll let him carry on.' Jesus rather asks about the spirit of the other's endeavours. How can the 'outsider' perform miracles in Jesus' name one minute and then say something bad about him in the next minute? 'Whoever is not against us is for us,' is his conclusion (Mark 9:38–40). It's that simple.

After Pentecost, a crisis looms in which the cultural annexation of 'the Way' by Jews who were believers in Christ threatens to limit the church simply to believers-in-Christ-via-Judaism. Peter has to experience a radical intervention by the Holy Spirit before it dawns on him that Gentiles could become as he is in Christ without having to become Jews first. Baptism of Cornelius' household in the Holy Spirit convinces Peter that he should baptise them all with water in the name of Jesus Christ. They are evidently Gentile 'Christians' and he hasn't even finished his sermon (Acts 10:44–46)!

Ten years later, Paul is vindicated at the Council of Jerusalem over the same issue. A group of faithful, persecuted Jewish Christians meet in the Holy City to decide whether the Holy Spirit is allowed to do what he is reportedly doing in Antioch. The wonder of this synod is that apostles and elders manage still to follow in the footsteps of their servant-Master. Who are they to stand in the path of God? It seems good to the Holy Spirit and to them to affirm the wonderful ministry going on in Antioch among non-Jews. They allow God to be God (Acts 15:6–29).

The 'fundamentalist' dye colours most of our human hearts, for it is an expression of our egocentricity. We would control even God if we could. The irony of the Islamists is that they so strongly believe that God himself authors what they do. Yet isn't that precisely the mark of all 'fundamentalisms'? The rest of mankind is to be forced to agree in the one divinely sanctioned view: 'our' view!

What a contrast with the self-emptying and vulnerability of incarnation! There, the momentum is in an opposite direction. What a risk the Word takes in becoming flesh! He may be misunderstood or misquoted. He may be excluded or his mission may be hijacked by those who think they know God's ways better than he. What embarrassment for the great Creator! He has sent an unsuccessful prophet, an ugly Man, a weak, despicable failure. Mere human beings bind him to a cross! Heaven must blush as even the Father withdraws from the Son: 'My God, why?...'

Yet that way, the way of the Lamb, is the key to the divine heart. The will of God, displayed in incarnation, crucifixion and resurrection reveals the character of God. The Creator loves his creation:

> Jesus asked a small child 'How much do you love me?'
> The child smiled back and replied 'Lots and lots.'
> Then the child asked Jesus 'How much do you love me?'
> Jesus stretched his arms out wide and tenderly said 'I love you this much.'
> Then they nailed him to the Cross.[62]

Childish still?

Our investigation of the worldview of the Muslim reformist certainly challenges those of us who have abandoned the possibility of public commitment to Christian 'truth' in our own Western culture and agreed in the secularising (and thus paganising) of our society. We have lost the wonder of seeing God as the mainspring and focal point of all life. We have enthroned ourselves and become masters of our own destinies. We have grown up outside of Christ and evolved into a mutated society: peripheral possibilities of faith but for most of life humanist in attitude. We need to take to heart the worldview of *tawḥîd* and search out ways in which Christ can be brought back into the centre of 'What all life is about' in the West.

It must, of course, be the Christ of the Gospels who is reinstated as Lord of all life in our Western world. The coercive Prophet of Islam, vindicated by his God in a triumphalist interpretation of 'submission', is not the model for Christians to emulate. To be on God's side will not necessarily require being always 'successful'! The struggle ahead of Western Christians is one of witness with its nuance of 'martyrdom', laying down our lives for the sake of others. The model to be emulated is that of Jesus Christ, incarnate Son of God, serving a lost world to the last breath of his life. Such service certainly included strong confrontation with centres of public power, with those who spoke for Caesar and with the religious status quo. In the strong confrontation in which Jesus was involved, however, attempts to control or manipulate the other party were conspicuously absent. Swords were to be put away. The inner attitude of a 'disciple' was as important as the case being made against an opponent. Trust in a righteous heavenly Father undergirded the Son's ministry on earth.

Our broader recognition of the phenomenon of 'fundamentalism' surely forces us to ask ourselves, highly motivated as we are, whether a similar spirit does not easily invade our outlook as 'witnesses for Christ'. We 'have' the truth as if God is in a box under our arm. We determine the manner in which others may become or be our brothers and sisters. We so crassly control the gentle Spirit of God, quenching, grieving, bruising him. Doves die easily!

Let's watch an infant eating a bit of sugar-icing 'Jesus' from a Coptic Epiphany cake. Can we see ourselves in that child? We are culture-bound, without a monopoly on God, gradually growing up in Christ, still not knowing him fully, yet convinced that he is happy for us to be who we are with him today. In the increasingly noisy war of worldviews we need to know, at the end of this study, that the future lies, not with the Islamists nor with us, but with the God and Father of our Lord Jesus Christ.

Heavenly Father,
We pray for your church which is set today
amid the perplexities of a changing order,
and is face to face with new challenges:
fill us afresh with the Spirit of Pentecost;
help us to bear witness to the coming of your kingdom;
and hasten the time when the knowledge of yourself
shall fill the earth as the waters cover the sea.

APPENDICES

TRANSLITERATION

A considerable number of non-English terms appear throughout this book. Italics have been used to indicate that a word is a transliteration, and does not appear as an English word in standard dictionaries. Some proper nouns have not been transliterated strictly, in order to ease reading. A glossary of all italicised transliterations is given in Appendix 3.

Most of the terms employed occur in Arabic. A standard form of transliteration, set out in Figure 25, has been used to express all Arabic expressions in English. A few words, such as 'Qur'ân' and 'ḥadîth', which do feature in some English dictionaries, are transliterated in this text.

Figure 25
Transliteration and pronunciation of Arabic alphabet

ARABIC NAME	SIGN USED	ENGLISH PRONUNCIATION WHERE UNCLEAR
hamza	'	glottal stop, as 'a' in 'apple'
âlif	*a*	
bâ'	*b*	
tâ'	*t*	
thâ'	*th*	as in 'think'
jîm	*j*	
ḥâ'	*ḥ*	(aspirated)

ARABIC NAME	SIGN USED	ENGLISH PRONUNCIATION WHERE UNCLEAR
khâ'	*kh*	as in German '*nacht*'
dâl	*d*	
dhâl	*dh*	as in 'this'
râ'	*r*	
zâ'	*z*	
sîn	*s*	
shîn	*sh*	as in 'shoe'
ṣâd	*ṣ*	(velarised)
ḍâd	*ḍ*	(velarised)
ṭâ'	*ṭ*	(velarised)
ẓâ'	*ẓ*	(velarised)
ʿayn	*ʿ*	voiced counterpart of *ha'*
ghayn	*gh*	similar to throaty French '*r*'
fâ'	*f*	
qâf	*q*	(uvular) as 'k', not 'kw'
kâf	*k*	(palatal)
lâm	*l*	
mîm	*m*	
nûn	*n*	
hâ'	*h*	
wâw	*w*	
yâ'	*y*	
âlif yâ	*ay*	(diphthong)
âlif wâw	*aw*	(diphthong)
tâ' marbûṭa	*a*	
unmarked (short) vowels are:	*a*	as in 'had'
	i	as in 'sit'
	u	as in 'fruit'
vowels with a circumflex above are long:	*â*	as in 'aah'
	î	as in 'eee'
	ô	as in 'ooo'

A short list, explaining some of the more significant, historical, Muslim names and movements, is also given at the end of the glossary in Appendix 3.

AN INTRODUCTORY BIBLIOGRAPHY

Worldview

Burnett, David. *Clash of Worlds*. MARC: Eastbourne, 1990.

Foster, George M. *Traditional Societies and Technological Change*. Harper and Row: San Francisco, 1973.

Hiebert, Paul G. *Cultural Anthropology*. J.B. Lippincott: Philadelphia, 1976.

Kearney, Michael. 'World View Theory and Study.' *Annual Review of Anthropology*. Vol 4 (1975): pp 247–270.

Krüger, J.S. *Studying Religion: A Methodological Introduction to Science of Religion*. University of South Africa: Pretoria, 1982.

Schneider, Louis (ed). *Religion, Culture and Society: A Reader in the Sociology of Religion*. John Wiley and Sons: New York, 1964.

Vrijhof, Pieter Hendrik and Waardenburg, Jacques (eds). *Official and Popular Religion: Analysis of a Theme for Religious Studies*. Mouton: The Hague, 1979.

Waardenburg, Jacques. *Reflections on the Study of Religion*. Mouton: The Hague, 1978.

Wallace, Anthony F.C. *Religion: An Anthropological View*. Random House: New York, 1966.

Islamic History and Political Thought

Cragg, Kenneth. *Counsels in Contemporary Islam*. Edinburgh University Press: Edinburgh, 1965.

Cragg, Kenneth. *The Pen and the Faith: Eight modern Muslim writers and the Qur'ân*. George Allen & Unwin: London, 1985.

Goldziher, Ignaz (Andras and Ruth Hamori trans, Bernard Lewis ed). *Introduction to Islamic Theology and Law*. Princeton University Press: Princeton, 1981.

Lapidus, Ira M. *A History of Islamic Societies*. Cambridge University Press: Cambridge, 1988.

Rahman, S.A. *Punishment of Apostasy in Islam*. Institute of Islamic Culture: Lahore, 1978.

Smith, Wilfred Cantwell. *Islam in Modern History*. Princeton University Press: Princeton, 1957.

Smith, Wilfred Cantwell. *On Understanding Islam: Selected Studies*. Mouton: The Hague, 1981.

Resurgent Islam

Donohue, John J. and Esposito, John L. (eds). *Islam in Transition: Muslim Perspectives*. Oxford University Press: New York, 1982.

Esposito, John L. (ed). *Voices of Resurgent Islam*. Oxford University Press: New York, 1983.

Geertz, Clifford. *Islam Observed: Religious Development in Morocco and Indonesia*. University of Chicago Press: Chicago, 1968.

Hiro, Dilip. *Islamic Fundamentalism*. Paladin Grafton Books: London, 1988.

Naipaul, V.S. *Among the Believers: An Islamic Journey*. Penguin Books: Harmondsworth, 1981.

Sadr, Allâma Muḥammad Bâqir Aṣ- (Shams C. Inati trans). *Our Philosophy*. The Muhammadi Trust & KPI: London, 1987.

Sarwar, Ghulam. *Islam: Beliefs and Teachings*. The Muslim Educational Trust: London, 1987.

Sivan, Emmanuel. *Radical Islam: Medieval Theology and Modern Politics*. Yale University Press: New Haven, 1985.

Egypt

Jansen, Johannes J.G. *The Neglected Duty: the Creed of Sadat's Assassins and Islamic Resurgence in the Middle East*. MacMillan: New York, 1986.

Kepel, Gilles (Jon Rothschild trans). *The Prophet and Pharaoh: Muslim Extremism in Egypt*. Al Saqi Books: London, 1985.

Mitchell, Richard P. *The Society of the Muslim Brothers*. Oxford University Press: London, 1969.

Qutb, Muhammad. *Islam and the Crisis of the Modern World*. Islamic Council of Europe: London, 1976.

Sadat, Anwar El (Thomas Graham trans). *Revolt on the Nile*. Allan Wingate: London, 1957.

Wendell, Charles (trans). *Five Tracts of Ḥasan al-Bannâ' (1906–1949): a Selection from the Majmû'at Rasâ'il al-Imâm al-Shahîd Ḥasan al-Bannâ'*. University of California Press: Berkeley, 1978.

Europe

Akhtar, Shabbir. *Be Careful with Muhammad! The Salman Rushdie Affair*. Bellew Publishing: London, 1989.

Gerholm, Tomas and Litman, Yngve Georg (eds). *The New Islamic Presence in Western Europe*. Mansell Publishing: London, 1988.

Nielsen, Jørgen S. (reporter). 'Islamic Law and its Significance for the Situation of Muslim Minorities in Europe.' *Research Papers*. No 35 (September 1987): pp 1–58.

Iran

Algar, Hamid (trans). *Islam and Revolution: Writings and Declarations of Imam Khomeini*. KPI Ltd: Berkeley, 1981.

Keddie, Nikki R. *Roots of Revolution: An Interpretive His-*

tory of Modern Iran. Yale University Press: New Haven, 1981.

Shariati, Ali (R. Campbell trans). *Marxism and Other Western Fallacies, an Islamic Critique*. Mizan Press: Berkeley, 1980.

Shariati, Ali (Hamid Algar trans). *On the Sociology of Islam*. Mizan Press: Berkeley, 1979.

Sprachman, Paul (trans). *Plagued by the West: Jalal Al-e-Ahmad's Gharbzadegi*. Caravan Books: New York, 1982.

Pakistan

Banuazizi, Ali and Weiner, Myron (eds). *The State, Religion and Ethnic Politics: Afghanistan, Iran and Pakistan*. Syracuse University Press: Syracuse, 1986.

Halliday, Fred and Alavi, Hamza (eds). *State and Ideology in the Middle East and Pakistan*. MacMillan Education: London, 1988.

Mawdudi, Abul A'la. *Towards Understanding Islam*. Islamic Foundation: Leicester, 1981.

Mintjes, H. *The Doctor and the Ladies. A New Debate on 'Women and Islam' in Pakistan*. Christian Study Centre: Rawalpindi, 1984.

Fundamentalism

Barr, James. *Fundamentalism*. Westminster Press: Philadelphia, 1978.

Barr, James. *Escaping from Fundamentalism*. SCM Press: London, 1984.

Caplan, Lionel (ed). *Studies in Religious Fundamentalism*. MacMillan Press: London, 1987.

Gill, Robin. *Competing Convictions*. SCM Press: London, 1989.

Lustick, Ian S. *For the Land and the Lord: Jewish Fundamentalism in Israel*. Council on Foreign Relations: New York, 1988.

Packer, James. *'Fundamentalism' and the Word of God*. William B. Eerdmans: Grand Rapids, 1958.

Western Culture

Dooyeweerd, Herman. *In the Twilight of Western Thought*. The Craig Press: Nutley, New Jersey, 1975.

Dooyeweerd, Herman (John Kraay trans). *Roots of Western Culture: Pagan, Secular and Christian Options*. Wedge Publishing Foundation: Toronto, 1979.

Goudzwaard, Bob (Josina Van Nuis Zylstra trans and ed). *Capitalism and Progress: A Diagnosis of Western Society*. Wedge Publishing Foundation: Toronto, 1979.

Newbigin, Lesslie. *The Gospel in a Pluralist Society*. SPCK: London, 1989.

Culture and Christian Mission

Anderson, J.N.D. *Christianity and Comparative Religion*. Inter-Varsity Press: London, 1970.

Chapman, Colin. *Whose Promised Land?* Lion: Tring, 1983.

Chapman, Colin. *'You Go and Do the Same': Studies in Relating to Muslims*. CMS, BMMF and IFES: London, 1983.

Cragg, Kenneth. *Jesus and the Muslim: An Exploration*. George Allen & Unwin: London, 1985.

Cragg, Kenneth. *The Christ and the Faiths: Theology in Cross-Reference*. SPCK: London, 1986.

Crooks, Peter. *Lebanon: The Pain and The Glory*. MARC: Eastbourne, 1990.

Good News in Our Times: The Gospel and Contemporary Cultures. Church House Publishing: London, 1991.

Hesselgrave, David J. *Communicating Christ Cross-Culturally*. Zondervan: Grand Rapids, 1978.

Hooker, Roger and Lamb, Christopher. *Love the Stranger: Christian Ministry in Multi-Faith Areas*. SPCK: London, 1986.

Jennings, George J. 'Islamic Culture and Christian

Missions.' *Practical Anthropology*. Vol 18, no 3 (1971): pp 128–144.

Kraft, Charles H. *Christianity in Culture: A Study in Dynamic Biblical Theologizing in Cross-Cultural Perspective*. Orbis Books: New York, 1979.

Loewen, Jacob A. *Culture and Human Values: Christian Intervention in Anthropological Perspective*. William Carey Library: Pasadena, 1975.

Luzbetak, Louis J. *The Church and Cultures*. Divine Word Publications: Techny, Illinois, 1963.

McGavran, Donald A. *The Clash Between Christianity and Cultures*. Canon Press: Washington, 1974.

Nazir-Ali, Michael. *Islam: A Christian Perspective*. The Paternoster Press: Exeter, 1983.

Neill, Stephen. *Christian Faith and Other Faiths: The Christian Dialogue with Other Religions*. Oxford University Press: Oxford, 1970.

Nida, Eugene A. *Customs and Cultures*. Harper and Row: New York, 1954.

Niebuhr, H. Reinhold. *Christ and Culture*. Harper and Brothers: New York, 1951.

Smalley, William A. (ed). *Missionary Anthropology*. William Carey Library: Pasadena, 1974.

Smalley, William A. (ed). *Readings in Missionary Anthropology II*. William Carey Library: Pasadena, 1978.

Sookhdeo, Patrick (ed). *Jesus Christ the Only Way: Christian Responsibility in a Multicultural Society*. Paternoster Press: Exeter, 1978.

Verkuyl, J. (Dale Cooper trans and ed). *Contemporary Missiology: An Introduction*. William B. Eerdmans: Grand Rapids, 1978.

GLOSSARY

Some significant terms used in the text

ʿadl: justice, Iran.

Aḥmadîya movement: developed in last quarter of nineteenth century in Indian Islam, named after Mirzâ Ghulâm Aḥmad; viewed as 'non-Islamic' in Pakistan since the Munir Report in 1954.

ʿAlids: descendants of the Prophet's cousin ʿAlî.

amâna: the trust of the earth delegated by God to men.

Amish: American Christians belonging to a strict Mennonite sect.

ʿÂshûrâ': 'the Tenth'; 10th day of Muḥarram, the first month in the Muslim calendar. On this day, Shîʿa Muslims bring to a conclusion their annual remembrance of Ḥusayn's murder at Karbalâ with a passion play and a procession often involving acts of self-flagellation.

Al-Azhar: ancient university mosque in Cairo, Egypt.

Badr: victorious battle fought by Prophet against Quraysh in AD 624 consolidating Muḥammad's power.

Chishti: Sufi order in India tracing their origin to Abû Isḥâq who settled at Chisht in Khurasan.

Companions: the *aṣḥâb* or associates of the Prophet Muḥammad. The general view is that everyone who embraced Islam, saw the Prophet and accompanied him was a 'Companion'.

dâr al-Ḥarb: 'the House of War'; territory not under Islamic law.

dâr al-Islâm: 'the House of Islam'; lands in which Islamic law prevails.

Dâr al-Islâmî: the name of Mawdudi's community in East Punjab prior to partition.

al-Da'wa: The Summons; name of newspaper published by the Muslim Brotherhood in Egypt.

al-dawla: 'dynasty'; government or state.

dhimmî: a non-Muslim citizen under Islamic rule.

al-dîn: 'religion'; religious practice in Islam.

farḍ: obligatory acts under Islamic law.

Al-Farîḍa al-Ghâ'iba: The Neglected Duty; book written by Faraj, an Egyptian Islamist ideologue who advocated the assassination of President Sadat.

fatwâ: legal opinion given by a *muftî.*

fiqh: 'understanding'; applied law.

fuqahâ': plural of *faqîh,* 'legist' and theologian; early writers of dogmatic theology. The *faqîh,* in Iran today, is the pious custodian of Islamic law who oversees the government of the nation.

ghâ'ibat: absence, Iran.

ḥadîth: (plural *aḥadîth*) 'prophetic tradition'; a short account of some word or act of Muhammad's. In its classic form it is passed on by one authority who has received it from another. The chain reaches back to an eyewitness.

ḥâfiz: 'a guardian'; a person who has memorised the whole of the Qur'ân.

ḥajj: 'setting out'; pilgrimage to Mecca and surrounding holy places.

ḥalâl: 'that which is loosed'; lawful.

ḥarâm: 'prohibited'; unlawful.

hijra: 'migration', hejira; date of Muhammad's flight from Mecca on the fourth day of the first month of AD 622. The Islamic calendar commences from the beginning of this year.

ḥizbullah: 'party of God'. In post-revolution Iran, *ḥizbullâhîs* (those of the party of God) exercised an informal form of repression in the country at large.

Hukumat-i Islami: Islamic Government; lectures given by Imam Khomeini in Najaf during 1970 and later published in one volume.

ḥusaynîya: centre for devotional rituals by Shî'as in remembrance of the martyrdom of al-Husayn.

ijmâ': 'consensus'; of legal scholars or Islamic community as a whole.

ijtihâd: 'exerting oneself'; individual initiative to reinterpret Islamic law or (in Shî'a Islam) to mediate it.

Al-Ikhwân al-Muslimûn: The Muslim Brotherhood; reformist group founded by Ḥasan al-Bannâ' in Egypt.

ilhâm: 'inspiration'; General Zia ul-Haq of Pakistan declared that he had experienced *ilhâm* in 1977 during which he was instructed by God to create an Islamic state.

imâm: leader of mosque prayer; *Imâm:* spiritual guide of Shî'a Muslims.

îmân: 'faith'; in the sense of a formal declaration of belief in the six articles of the Muslim creed.

intizar: expectation of the Mahdî's advent, Iran.

islâh: purification and revitalisation of Muslim community by return to basic principles of Qur'ân and *sunna*.

Islâmî-Jamâ'at-i Ṭulâba: Islamic Student Organisation, the youth wing of the *Jamâ'at-i Islâmî* in Pakistan.

'ismat: purity, Iran.

isnâd: chain of transmitters (of *hadîth*) going back to Companions of the Prophet.

istidlâl: term used in science of exegesis for those sentences of the Qur'ân needing certain proofs.

istiḥsân: 'approving'; part of science of exegesis in which expediency is approved over the principle of *qiyâs*.

istiṣlâḥ: legal position validated on grounds of public welfare.

jâhilî: sphere of 'ignorance'; Islamists speak of it in contrast with the separated, reformist cell where true Islam is adhered to.

jâhilîya: the days of ignorance in Arabia before Islam. Contemporary Islamists use the term to refer to the days of adulterated Islam existing in most Muslim countries prior to resurgence.

jama'a: 'assembly'; the community of true believers.

Jamâ'at-i Islâmî: The Islamic Organisation, founded by Mawdudi.

Jamâ'at Islamîya: Islamic Associations, proliferating in Egypt during Sadat's presidency.

Jamâ'at al-Muslimûn: Society of the Muslims; militant Islamist group active in Egypt during the 1970s.

Jami'at al-'Ulama-i Hind: Association of the Ulema of India.

jihâd: 'a striving'; religious war of Muslims against unbelievers or apostates.

jizya: the tax payable by *dhimmîs*.

jund: soldier, army.

ka'ba: 'a cube'; the cube-like building in the centre of the Sacred Mosque at Mecca. It contains the black stone.

Al-Kabîr: a well-known collection of *hadîth* written by Sulaymân ibn Ahmad al-Tabarânî (AD 873–971), a Syrian.

kalima: 'the word'; the creed of the Muslim.

kalimât al-shahâda: 'the word of testimony'; the confession: 'I bear witness that there is no deity but God, and that Muhammad is his apostle.'

Karbalâ': city in Iraq, celebrated as the site of the martyrdom of al-Husayn.

khalîfa: 'caliph'; successor of the Prophet and head of the Muslim community.

khilâfa: politically, the succession to the rule of the community; theologically it means the status of Adam, man as trustee for God in the world.

Ma'âlim Fî'l-Tarîq: Signposts on the Road, written by Sayyid Qutb.

madhhab: a Muslim school of law, there being four principal ones.

Mahdî: the 'directed one'; a ruler to appear on earth in the last days.

makrûh: 'that which is unbecoming'; improper, according to Islamic law.

Al-Manâr: The Minaret (literally 'The Lighthouse'); journal of the *Salafîya* movement.

mandûb: actions which are 'recommended' in Islamic law.

ma'rifa: 'insight'; mystical awareness of reality.

matn: the substance of a *hadîth*, as distinct from its *isnâd*.

mawlânâ: from 'protector'; official versed in Islamic theology, Pakistan.

Mawlid al-Nabî: 'Birthday of the Prophet'; 12th of Rabî' al-Awwal.

Milli Selamet Partisi: National Salvation Party; Turkish political party urging Islamist philosophy. Formed in 1972, it is a continuation of the National (Islamic) Order Party (*Milli Nizam Partisi*) and constitutes the third largest party in the country.

Mogul: empire established in India in AD 1526 by Babar, a prince from what is now Afghanistan. The Mogul Empire began to break up after the death of Aurangzeb in 1707. Moguls continued to rule a small kingdom at Delhi until Great Britain took control of India in the 1800s.

mubâh: 'silent'; actions allowed or neutral in Islamic law.

muftî: expert in Islamic law qualified to give legal opinions.

muhyî al-dîn: 'renewer of religion'; individual expected in each age who precipitates renewal of Muslim community (Sunnî).

mujahideen: from *mujahid*, 'warrior'; Islamic fighters.

mujtahid: person qualified to exercise *ijtihâd*.

Munazzamat al-Jihâd: The Jihad Organisation; Islamist group in Egypt responsible for the assassination of President Sadat.

murshid: 'guide'; spiritual director, especially in Pakistan and India; in Egypt applied to Ḥasan al-Bannâ' as leader of the Muslim Brotherhood.

Musnad: collection of *ḥadîth* made by Imâm Aḥmad ibn Ḥanbal.

mustazafîn: needy, oppressed, Iran.

al-nâs: 'the people'; the mass in Shariati's interpretation of the Qur'ân.

al-niẓâm al-islâmî: the Islamic system of ordering life, promoted by Ḥasan al-Bannâ'.

niẓâm-i Mustafa: the political system of the Prophet Muḥammad; slogan proposed by Islamic groups in Pakistan in opposition to Bhutto.

pancasila: 'five principles' of nationhood, designed to order inter-action of five different religious groups in Indonesia: Muslims, Catholics, Protestants, Buddhists and Hindus.

Pahlavi: Iranian dynasty, 1925–1979, under the Shahs.

qâdî: judge; caliph's designated representative to judge disputes on basis of Islamic law.

Qâ'id-i ʿAzam: Great Founder; refers to Muḥammad ʿAlî Jinnâḥ.

qiyâs: 'comparison'; analogical principle whereby Islamic law may be extended to situations not exactly covered in the Qur'ân or *sunna*.

Quraysh: the Arabian tribe of which Muḥammad was a part and to which the majority of Meccans belonged.

Râj: 'reign' (Hindi); the British rule in India.

Ramaḍân: the fast during the ninth month of the Muslim calendar.

ra'y: 'view'; opinion held in the process of *ijtihâd*.

ridda: 'apostasy' from Islam.

Safavids: rulers of a Persian Empire AD 1499–1736.

Saʿîdî: person living in the Saʿid, the south of Egypt.

Salafîya movement: founded by Muhammad ʿAbduh in Egypt, promoting *islâh* and national identity.

ṣalât: ritual or liturgical prayer, performed five times a day.

SAVAK/SAVAMA: acronyms for Iranian secret police under Shah/Islamic Republic.

Shabâb Muḥammad: the People of Muḥammad; Islamist movement that broke away from Muslim Brotherhood in Egypt in 1939.

shahîd: 'martyr'; with sense of 'witness unto death'.

sharî'a: the 'path' to be followed; the totality of the Islamic way of life.

shaykh: 'sheikh'; Muslim religious leader, sometimes head of an order.

Shî'a: 'followers'; followers of 'Alî, first cousin of Muḥammad and the husband of his daughter Fâṭima.

Shuddhi movement: Hindu movement in India in early twentieth century with goal to reconvert to Hinduism some of the depressed classes of India who were only nominally Muslim.

siyâsa: politics.

Ṣûfi: Sufi; a Muslim mystic, named after the early ascetics who wore garments of coarse wool.

sunna: 'a path, manner of life'; the custom, especially of Muḥammad, transmitted via the *hadîth* literature.

Sunnî: those who accept the *sunna* and the historic succession of the caliphs, as opposed to the 'Alids or Shî'as; the majority of the Muslim community.

sura: from *sûra,* 'a row or series'; chapter of the Qur'ân.

tafsîr: 'explaining'; term used for commentary, especially on the Qur'ân.

Tahrir Islâmî: Islamic Liberation; Islamist group in Egypt strong in the 1970s.

Al-Takfir wa'l-Hijra: The Denunciation and the Migration; nickname used by Egyptian authorities for *Jamâ'at al-Muslimûn* (Society of the Muslims), an Islamist group active in Egypt in the 1970s.

tajdîd: 'renewal'; applied to post-eighteenth-century movement to revive Islam based on fidelity to Qur'ân and *hadîth.*

tanzîl: movement of revelation in Islam; causing to 'come down'.

taqlîd: 'imitation', Iran; often with sense of blind adherence to a traditional school and non-openness to renewal.

ṭarîqa: 'a path'; Sufi term for the religious life. Often describes the division of mystics into different lodges.

Tarjumân al-Qur'ân: Exegesis of the Qur'ân; journal edited by Mawdudi.

tawḥîd: 'unity'; the oneness of God and, by implication, the holism of all creation in realising its theocentric nature.

Taoist: follower of Taoism, religious doctrine originally based on writings attributed to Lao-tse, Chinese philosopher (circa 500 BC).

'ulamâ': plural of *'âlim*, 'knower'; learned ones who are custodians of Islamic teachings.

Umayyad: Umayyad caliphate AD 661–750 with capital at Damascus.

umma: the 'community' of Islam; the whole of the brotherhood of Muslims.

vilayat: governance, Iran.

vilayat al-faqîh: governance of the *faqîh*, the expert in the law, Iran.

visayat: designation of authority, Iran.

Wafd: 'arrival'; refers to party in Egypt prominent prior to the revolution in 1952.

zakât: 'purification'; alms-giving, one of the five pillars.

Some significant names mentioned in the text

'Abduh: Muḥammad (1849–1905). *Muftî* of Egypt from 1889 to 1905; sought to reformulate Islam, preserving the fundamentals and discarding various historical accretions. His Islamic reformism inspired the *Salafîya* movement in the Middle East and North Africa.

al-Afghânî: Jamâl al-Dîn (1839–1897). Educated as a Shî'a; sought to warn Muslims about the threat of European subjugation. Reformation of corrupt Muslim societies would provide groundwork for solidarity against the European powers.

Ahmad: Jalal Al-e (1923–1969). Iranian moral polemicist who wrote in popular mode seeking to negate the influence of Westernism in Iranian society during the Shah's regime. Clandestine printings of his work were distributed; after the revolution his material flooded bookshops and bookstalls throughout Iran.

Al-Bukhârî: Muḥammad Ibn 'Abd Allâh Ibn Ismâ'îl (810–870). Major collator of *ḥadîth* whose collection is approved as a work second only to the Qur'ân itself.

Ḥanbal: Aḥmad ibn (780–855). Founder of the Hanbalite school of Sunnî law, the most strict school.

Ḥanîfa: Abû Ḥanîfa al-Nu'mân (700–767). Founder of Hanifite school of Sunnî law.

al-Ḥudaybi: Ḥasan Ismâ'îl. Former Egyptian judge who succeeded Ḥasan al-Bannâ' as leader of the Muslim Brotherhood.

Iqbâl: Sir Muḥammad (1876–1938). Probably the most prominent spokesman of Indian Muslims in the twentieth century; also composer of passionate religious and moral poetry. Spoke out in 1930 in favour of a Muslim homeland.

Jinnâḥ: Muḥammad 'Alî (1876–1948). Spokesman for the Muslim League in India, at first demanding a federal Indian state with autonomous Muslim provinces, later calling for a separate Muslim homeland.

Mâlik: Abû 'Abd Allâh Mâlik ibn Anas (716–796). Medinan founder of the Malikite school of Sunnî law.

Mussaddiq: Muḥammad. Prime Minister of Iran 1951–1953; led struggle against the British oil company's (BP) monopoly of oil production and pricing.

Nuqrashi Pasha: Maḥmûd Fahmi. Prime Minister of Egypt who was assassinated by a member of the Muslim Brotherhood in December 1948. The authorities retaliated by killing Ḥasan al-Bannâ'.

Riḍâ: Rashîd (1865–1935). A disciple of Muḥammad 'Abduh, he interpreted the *Salafîya* movement in a conservative sense in his native Syria. He emphasised opposition to Shî'a Islam and Sufi shrines.

Shâfi'î: Muḥammad ibn Idrîs al-Shâfi'î (767–820). Descendant of Prophet and founder of one of the four schools of Sunnî law.

Ibn Taimîya: Taqî al-Dîn Ibn Taimîya (1263–1328) emerged as spokesman for the traditionalists (*Ahl al-Ḥadîth*) with a programme of renewed emphasis on the *sharî'a* (Islamic law) and a vindication of religious values. He spoke out strongly against the many forms of popular practices prevalent among his peers. Ibn Taimîya's thoughts influenced the late eighteenth-century Wahhâbî movement.

'Uthmân: son of 'Affân; the third *khalîfa* of Islam. During his rule, a definitive text of the Qur'ân was determined and authorised, all other versions being destroyed.

Wahhâb: Muḥammad Ibn 'Abdu'l-Wahhâb (1703–1792) was a native of Najd in Arabia, and founded the unitarian, conservative movement named after him. The Wahhâbî view influenced the development of the Muslim Brotherhood in Egypt, and the *Jamâ'at-i Islâmî* or Islamic Organisation in Pakistan.

APPENDIX FOUR

NOTES

[1] Epiphany: the Greek original means 'manifestation'. Epiphany is a feast of the church originating in the East in which the nativity of Christ (ie, his 'manifestation' to mankind) or, more often, his baptism, is celebrated. In the West, it has come to be associated with the manifestation of Christ to the Gentiles, celebrating the visit of the Magi who are assumed to be the first Gentile believers.

[2] For an in-depth study of the concept of worldview and its implications for Christian mission, see David Burnett, *Clash of Worlds* (MARC, Eastbourne, 1990).

[3] The Fifth Amendment to the Constitution of the United States of America, entitled 'Rights in Criminal Cases', declares that 'no person shall be...deprived of life, liberty, or property, without due process of law'. The same words occur in the Fourteenth Amendment on 'Civil Rights'. The phrase expresses the idea that a person's life, liberty and property are not subject to the uncontrolled power of the government.

[4] 'Ali Shari'ati in 'The World-View of Tauhid' in *On the Sociology of Islam*, translated by Hamid Algar (Mizan Press: Berkeley, 1979), p 82.

5 Illustrated on page 113 of this book.

6 Quoted in A.J. Arberry (ed), *Aspects of Islamic Civilization* (The University of Michigan Press: Ann Arbor, 1964), p 381.

7 *The World Book Encyclopedia* (World Book—Childcraft International Inc: Chicago, 1980), vol 8, p 336.

8 See Jamâl al-Dîn al-Afghânî on 'An Islamic Response to Imperialism', quoted in John J. Donohue and John L. Esposito (eds), *Islam in Transition: Muslim Perspectives* (Oxford University Press: New York, 1982), pp 16–19.

9 The word 'Shî'a' means 'sect' but functions as a generic term for a variety of groups who hold that the Imamate is essential in Islam. The Imamate, or leadership, of the Muslim community is passed on, in the Shî'a view, through the line of Muhammad's son-in-law, 'Alî. 'Alî, the nearest surviving male relative of the Prophet Muhammad, was the first *Imâm*, according to the Shî'as. This idea of a passing down of 'the light of Muhammad', rather like a glorious equivalent of the Christian concept of 'apostolic succession', means that the Shî'as reject the first three caliphs (recognised by Sunnî Muslims) as usurpers and hold that 'Alî should have been the first caliph. The split originated in a fight over the leadership of the Muslim community at the end of the seventh century AD. The Prophet's grandson ('Alî's son) and his family were cruelly murdered at Karbalâ by the forces of Yazîd who thereby consolidated his own (Umayyad) dynasty, centred on Damascus. In various degrees of extremity, the Shî'a accord the *Imâms* divine status. The major Shî'a population in today's Muslim world is found in Iran. See Chapter Seventeen for further details of the concept of the Imamate in Shî'a society.

10 Known in the West as Ayatollah Khomeini, but elevated to the title of Imam by Iranian Muslims during the revolution.

11 Muhammad Zia ul-Haq on the 'Introduction of the

Islamic System in Pakistan' quoted in Donohue and Esposito, *op cit*, p 273.

[12] See General Zia ul-Haq's words recorded in *The Pakistan Times* (6 July 1977), quoted in H. Mintjes, *The Doctor and the Ladies: A New Debate on 'Women and Islam' in Pakistan* (Christian Study Centre: Rawalpindi, 1984), p 13.

[13] From Khurshid Ahmad (ed), *Islamic Law and Constitution* (Islamic Publications: Lahore, 1967), p 109.

[14] Summarised from Professor Abû'l-ʿAlâ' al-Mawdûdî, 'The Rights of Minorities in an Islamic State', published in *Tarjumân al-Qur'ân* (1948), translated by R. Bellani and printed in *Encounter* no 64 (1980): pp 17–19.

[15] See Brian Lapping in *End of Empire* (Granada Publishing Limited: London, 1985), pp 69–103.

[16] From G.W. Choudhury (ed), *Documents and Speeches on the Constitution of Pakistan* (Dacca, 1967), pp 21f, quoted in Hamza Alavi 'Pakistan and Islam: Ethnicity and Ideology' in Fred Halliday and Hamza Alavi (eds), *State and Ideology in the Middle East and Pakistan* (MacMillan Education: Basingstoke, 1988), p 104.

[17] See Mintjes, *op cit*, for documentation of this controversy.

[18] From 'To What Do We Summon Mankind?' in Ḥasan Al-Bannâ', *Five Tracts of Ḥasan Al-Bannâ'* (1906–1949). A Selection from the *Majmûʿat Rasâ'il al-Imâm al-Shahîd Ḥasan al-Bannâ'*, translated by Charles Wendell (University of California Press: Berkeley, 1978), p 87.

[19] Summarised from 'On Jihad' in Ḥasan Al-Bannâ', *Five Tracts of Ḥasan Al-Bannâ'* (1906–1949). A Selection from the *Majmûʿat Rasâ'il al-Imâm al-Shahîd Ḥasan al-Bannâ'*, translated by Charles Wendell (University of California Press: Berkeley, 1978), pp 133–161.

20 *Ibid*, p 156.

21 See Chapter Five, p 56 on Jamâl al-Dîn al-Afghânî and Muḥammad ʿAbduh.

22 Quoted in Richard P. Mitchell, *The Society of the Muslim Brothers* (Oxford University Press: London, 1969), pp 86f.

23 Anwar El Sadat, *Revolt on the Nile*, translated by Thomas Graham (Allan Wingate: London, 1957), pp 27f.

24 Sayyid Qutb, *Fî Ẓilâl al-Qurʾân* (*Dâr al-Shurûq:* Beirut, 1973–74), vol 1, p 108, quoted in Yvonne Y. Haddad, 'Sayyid Qutb: Ideologue of Islamic Revival' in John L. Esposito (ed), *Voices of Resurgent Islam* (OUP: New York, 1983), p 80.

25 Sayyid Qutb, *Maʿâlim fîʾl-Tarîq* (*Maktabat Wahbah*: Cairo, 1964), p 93, quoted in Yvonne Y. Haddad, *op cit*, p 82.

26 From *Al-Ahram* (4, 5 February 1966), translated and quoted by Emmanuel Sivan, *Radical Islam: Medieval Theology and Modern Politics* (Yale University Press: New Haven, 1985), pp 85f.

27 Quoted in Richard P. Mitchell, *op cit*, p 156.

28 Perhaps better translated '*The Missing Precept*'. An English translation of *Al-Farîḍa al-Ghâʾiba* is found in Johannes J.G. Jansen, *The Neglected Duty: The Creed of Sadat's Assassins and Islamic Resurgence in the Middle East* (MacMillan: New York, 1986), pp 159–234.

29 In Ali Shariʾati, *Marxism and Other Western Fallacies*, translated by R. Campbell (Mizan Press: Berkeley, 1980), p 95.

30 *Ibid*, p 96.

31 Ali Shariati, *Tashayyoʾ-e ʾalavi va tashayyoʾ-e safavi* (np, nd), reproduced and summarised in Nikki R. Keddie, *Roots*

of Revolution: An Interpretive History of Modern Iran (Yale University Press: New Haven, 1981), pp 218–220. Used with permission.

[32] M. Azarm (Nemat Mirzazadeh), *Be Nameto Sogand*, translated by Mehdi Abedi from text in *Zendigi-Nameh Imam Khomeini* (Fifteen of Khordad Publishers: Teheran, nd), vol II, p 1, quoted in Michael M.J. Fischer, 'Imam Khomeini: Four Levels of Understanding' in John L. Esposito (ed), *Voices of Resurgent Islam* (OUP: New York, 1983), p 150.

[33] From Imam Khomeini's speech on 3 June 1963, tenth of Muḥarram, quoted in Fischer, *op cit*, p 155.

[34] Imam Khomeini, 'The First Day of God's Government', found in *Islam and Revolution: Writings and Declarations, Imam Khomeini*, translated by Hamid Algar (KPI Ltd: London, 1981), p 266.

[35] Imam Khomeini, 'The Form of Islamic Government', from *Islamic Government* found in *Islam and Revolution*, p 55.

[36] Imam Khomeini, 'Program for the Establishment of an Islamic Government', from *Islamic Government*, found in *Islam and Revolution*, pp 137f.

[37] *Ibid*, p 146.

[38] From Imam Khomeini's speech in 1979 on the anniversary of the Black Friday (8 September 1978) *Jaleh* Square massacre. Quoted in Fischer, *op cit*, p 168.

[39] A translation of Jalal Al-e Ahmad's *Gharbzadegi* is found in Paul Sprachman (trans), *Plagued by the West* (Caravan Books: New York, 1981).

[40] Shî'a Islam sees a vital link between each generation and Prophet Muḥammad through the *Imâms*, starting with ʿAlî, son-in-law of the Prophet (see note [9] above). Some Shî'as

count five, some seven and some twelve, *Imâms* in the succession. A common conviction is that the last of these respective *Imâms* was 'occulted' or concealed, hidden until God should choose to manifest him to guide the faithful once more. From concealment the *Imâm* preserves his people in the truth faith, most significantly via special representatives on earth.

[41] Quoted in Dilip Hiro, *Islamic Fundamentalism* (Paladin Grafton Books: London, 1988), pp 172f.

[42] From Imam Khomeini's Christmas Message 1979, quoted in Hasan Askari 'Khomeini and Non-Muslims' in *Encounter*, no 71 (1981): p 6.

[43] Quoted in Askari, *op cit*, p 8.

[44] See Appendix 1 in Bill Musk, *The Unseen Face of Islam* (MARC, Evangelical Missionary Alliance: Eastbourne, 1989) for an explanation of the *hadîth* literature.

[45] See note [40] concerning the 'Hidden *Imâm*'.

[46] Ghulam Sarwar, *Islam: Belief and Teachings* (The Muslim Educational Trust: London, 1980), p 164.

[47] These paragraphs are not intended to constitute a detailed analysis of the related concepts of revelation, inspiration and 'Scripture'. They are intended to demonstrate something of the difference between the deliberately literalist approach entailed in the Islamic doctrine of *tanzîl* and the 'human co-operation' nuance of the biblical position.

[48] Shabbir Akhtar, *Be Careful with Muhammad: The Salman Rushdie Affair* (Bellew Publishing: London, 1989), p 98.

[49] Salman Rushdie, *The Satanic Verses* (Viking: London, 1988), p 123.

[50] Shî'a Muslims have tended to claim that the 'Uthmân recension comprises an adjusted version: 'Alî's name does

not appear in it and other explicit Shîʿa emphases are missing. Sometimes it is alleged that two suras are missing which originally gave more authentication to Shîʿa concerns. The major difference between Sunnî and Shîʿa erupts, however, over details of interpretation of the Qur'ân.

51 In the early history of Islam, the Muʿtazila (literally 'the Separatists') held, among other non-orthodox views, that the Word of God was not eternal but created.

52 For surveys of the variety of challenges facing Muslims in different countries of the world, and for samples of the variety of responses being made to those challenges by different kinds of Muslims, see Wilfred Cantwell Smith, *Islam in Modern History* (Princeton University Press: Princeton, 1957) and Kenneth Cragg, *Counsels in Contemporary Islam* (Edinburgh University Press: Edinburgh, 1965).

53 See, for example, the material presented on 'The Application of the *Sharîʿa* in Egypt' in Donohue and Esposito, *op cit*, pp 238–250.

54 See Chapter Six, p 73.

55 Muḥammad bin Ismâʿîl bin al-Mughîrah al-Bukhârî, *Ṣahîh*, translated by Muḥammad Muhsin Khan (Kazi Publications: Chicago, 1979), vol VIII, chapters 1-4, pp 519–522.

56 Khurshid Ahmad, 'The Nature of the Islamic Resurgence' in Esposito, *Voices of Resurgent Islam*, p 228.

57 From the record of an interview with Imam Khomeini under the title 'The Religious Scholars Led the Revolt' in *Islam and Revolution*, p 341.

58 From the record of a speech by Imam Khomeini on 8 January 1978 under the title 'In Commemoration of the First Martyrs of the Revolution', in *Islam and Revolution*, p 219.

59 Bishop Lesslie Newbigin, 'Muslims, Christians and Public Doctrine', in *The Gospel and Our Culture*, no 6 (1990): p 2.

[60] See Ian S. Lustick, *For the Land and the Lord: Jewish Fundamentalism in Israel* (Council on Foreign Relations: New York, 1988).

[61] Kenneth Cragg, *Jesus and the Muslim: An Exploration* (George Allen & Unwin: London, 1985), p 285.

[62] 'Thought for the Day', quoted in Tony Castle, *'Quotations for All Occasions'* (Marshall Pickering: London, 1989), p 203.